A

Law

Emma Bradbury

ESSENTIAL WORD
DICTIONARY

Philip Allan Updates, part of the Hodder Education Group, an Hachette Livre UK company, Market Place, Deddington, Oxfordshire OX15 0SE

Orders
Bookpoint Ltd, 130 Milton Park, Abingdon, Oxfordshire, OX14 4SB
tel: 01235 827720
fax: 01235 400454
e-mail: uk.orders@bookpoint.co.uk
Lines are open 9.00 a.m.–5.00 p.m., Monday to Saturday, with a 24-hour message answering service. You can also order through the Philip Allan Updates website: www.philipallan.co.uk

© Philip Allan Updates 2007

ISBN 978-0-86003-387-5

First printed 2007
Impression number 5 4 3 2 1
Year 2012 2011 2010 2009 2008 2007

Printed in Malta

Philip Allan Updates' policy is to use papers that are natural, renewable and recyclable products and made from wood grown in sustainable forests. The logging and manufacturing processes are expected to conform to the environmental regulations of the country of origin.

Introduction

This *Essential Word Dictionary* defines the words and phrases used in AS and A2 law. It is intended to be a quick reference guide to legal terminology.

The majority of definitions relate to the English legal system, crime and tort. The main terms relating to morality, contract law and human rights are included, as well as other legal terms where necessary. Important case law is also defined.

The definitions may include an example and/or a useful tip. Throughout the dictionary there are cross-references to words and phrases defined elsewhere, which are shown in this *italic* font.

This dictionary has been written to fulfil the criteria of AS and A2 law. It contains terms that you might come across in the course of your studies at this level. Other law dictionaries are available, but many are aimed at an undergraduate market and therefore contain terms that you will not need. Use this dictionary to check your knowledge of terminology and to ensure that your essays are accurate and comprehensive.

abatement notice: issued by a local authority to stop a *statutory nuisance*.
- Failure to comply with the notice can result in a *fine* being issued by the *Magistrates' Court*.

abatement of liability: the *defendant* deceives the victim into letting him or her not pay in the future.

abet (*secondary participation*): to incite, instigate or encourage the performance of a crime either before or during its commission.
- There does not have to be a causative link between the actions of the abettor and the offence committed by the *principal offender*.

ABH: see *actual bodily harm*.

abnormality of mind (*diminished responsibility*): described by Lord Parker in *R v Byrne (1960)*, as 'a state of mind so different from that of ordinary people that the reasonable person would term it abnormal'.
- This is a matter for the *jury* to decide in each case, based on the medical evidence submitted by both the defence and *prosecution*.

abnormal sensitivity (*private nuisance*): a *claimant* cannot put his or her *land* to an unusually delicate use and then complain when that land is adversely affected by a neighbour's activities to a greater extent than would usually be the case.
- *e.g.* In *Robinson* v *Kilvert* (1889), the claimant used the ground floor of a building to store special paper. In the cellar below, the *defendant* made cardboard boxes, which required the room to be kept warm in order to dry the glue used in the process. The heat from the cellar damaged the claimant's paper. However, the heat from the cellar was not unreasonable and normal paper would not have been damaged, so the claim failed.
- If the nuisance causes general *damage* to the claimant's use and enjoyment of land, a claim for damage to something abnormally sensitive is allowed (*McKinnon Industries* v *Walker*, 1951).

absolute liability: the *defendant* is liable if he or she performed the *actus reus*, whether voluntarily or involuntarily.
- Unlike *strict liability*, the prosecution does not need to prove that the defendant was acting voluntarily, so even an involuntary act would incur liability. Few

a

offences fall into this category, and those that do must be clearly defined as such (e.g. *R v Larsonneur, 1933*).

acceptance: agreement to the terms of an *offer*, the second requirement of a valid *contract*.

■ The acceptance must be on the exact terms of the offer (a mirror image); if not, it is a *counter-offer*. Once an offer has been made, the *offeree* may accept in writing, orally or by his or her conduct (silence does not constitute acceptance). Acceptance by letter is treated as communicated when the letter is posted (rather than on the day it is received) — *Adams* v *Lindsell* (1818). This is known as the *postal rule*. Contracts made using the telephone or fax machine are accepted when they are communicated to the *offeror*.

accessory (also known as an accomplice)**:** a person who is involved in the commission of a crime by *aiding, abetting, counselling* or *procuring* the principal offender.

■ *TIP* An accessory to *murder* will receive the same sentence as the *principal offender*.

Access to Justice Report 1996: *Lord Woolf's* criticisms of the *civil court* system and his suggested proposals for how to improve it.

■ The *County Court* and *High Court* had different procedures, which were complicated and expensive. Cases would suffer delays, which would in turn cause more expense to the parties involved. The report found that the procedures were too adversarial and did not promote *alternative dispute resolution*, there was too much emphasis on oral evidence, and the whole process of making a claim was too driven by *lawyers*. The *Civil Procedure Rules 1999* were implemented as a result of the report.

accomplice: see *accessory*.

accused (also known as the *defendant*)**:** the person on trial for a crime.

actionable *per se*: refers to a *civil law* claim that is allowed without the *claimant* having suffered any *damage*.

■ *e.g.* *Trespass to land* and *false imprisonment* do not require any harm to have occurred for a claim to be successful.

action plan order (*young offender*)**:** a youth community order requiring a child or young person to comply with a 3-month programme that is individually tailored to the young offender in question and which addresses the specific underlying causes of his or her offences.

■ It aims to rehabilitate the young offender and may involve taking part in activities focused on *reparation*, going to an attendance centre or undertaking educational programmes.

Act of Parliament (also known as statutory law or a statute)**:** a law made by *Parliament*.

■ An Act of Parliament starts off as a *bill* and has to pass through the various stages of the *legislation* process, involving the *House of Commons*, the *House of Lords* and the queen (*royal assent*).

■ Also see *supremacy of Parliament*.

actual bodily harm (ABH): assault occasioning actual bodily harm is an offence under s.47 of the *Offences Against the Person Act 1861* as: 'any assault occasioning actual bodily harm'.

■ This is an *either-way offence* and carries a maximum sentence of 5 years' imprisonment.

■ The *actus reus* of ABH has been interpreted as being committed with either *assault* or *battery*. In addition, the prosecution must use the rules of *causation* to prove that the *assault* or *battery* caused ABH.

■ ABH has been given a wide definition. In *R v Miller* (1954), the court stated: 'Actual bodily harm includes any hurt or injury calculated to interfere with the health or comfort of the prosecutor.' Thus ABH can occur where discomfort to the person is caused. However, in *R v Chan-Fook* (1994) Lord Justice Hobhouse said in the *Court of Appeal*: 'The word "actual" indicates that the injury (although there is no need for it to be permanent) should not be so trivial as to be wholly insignificant.'

■ ABH can include *psychiatric injury/nervous shock*, but not mere emotions such as fear, distress or panic. The injury must be an identifiable clinical condition (see *R v Ireland, R v Burstow, 1997*).

■ The *mens rea* for ABH is the same as that for assault and battery. No additional *mens rea* is required (see *R v Roberts, 1978*).

***actus reus*:** Latin for 'guilty act'.

■ The *actus reus* is made up of all of the parts of the crime except the *defendant's* mental state (*mens rea*). There are several different types of *actus reus*, including prohibited conduct (*conduct crime*), a *state of affairs*, a specified consequence (*result crime*) and an *omission* to act.

adjournment: the postponement of legal proceedings until a later date.

ADR: see *alternative dispute resolution*.

advocacy: speaking on behalf of another.

■ Legal professionals do this on behalf of their clients in court cases.

■ Traditionally, *barristers* have specialised in advocacy — representing clients in court in both criminal and civil cases.

■ *Solicitors* can represent their clients in the *Magistrates' Court* and the *County Court*. Since the *Courts and Legal Services Act 1990*, solicitors can pass an exam called the Certificate of Advocacy that allows them to represent their clients in the higher courts. Such solicitors are known as solicitor advocates.

Advocates General: senior law officers who assist the *judges* in the *European Court of Justice* by researching the cases sent to the court and producing written opinions.

affidavit: a written statement of evidence that is signed on oath or affirmed as being true before a person authorised to take oaths in respect of the particular type of affidavit.

a

affirmative resolution procedure: a vote taken by *Parliament* to pass *delegated legislation* that involves important or constitutional powers.

affray: defined in s.3 of the *Public Order Act 1986* as using or threatening unlawful violence towards another so as to cause a person of reasonable firmness present at the scene to fear for his or her personal safety.

■ This offence can be committed in public or in private and no person of reasonable firmness actually needs to be present. The threat must be more than verbal.

■ The maximum sentence for affray is 3 years' *imprisonment* and a *fine*.

age of discretion (*Coke's definition of murder*)**:** as with other crimes, to be charged with *murder* the defendant must be over the age of 10.

■ This is known as the *doli incapax* rule.

aggravated criminal damage: offence defined in s.1(2) of the *Criminal Damage Act 1971*:

> A person who without lawful excuse destroys or damages any property, whether belonging to himself or another:
>
> (a) intending to destroy or damage any property or being reckless as to whether any property would be destroyed or damaged; and
>
> (b) intending by the destruction or damage to endanger the life of another or being reckless as to whether the life of another would be thereby endangered shall be guilty of an offence.

■ This is similar to the offence of *criminal damage* but allows for the property that is damaged to belong to the *defendant*.

■ *TIP* This offence has a maximum sentence of life imprisonment.

aggravated damages: increased *damages* awarded in a civil case when the conduct of the *defendant* has aggravated the *claimant's* injuries.

■ *e.g.* According to Lord Devlin in *Rookes* v *Barnard* (1964), this includes humiliating the claimant or acting out of spite.

aggravating factors: these make an offence more serious and can result in a more severe sentence being passed.

■ *e.g.* Aggravating factors can include: if a weapon was used; if an attack was premeditated; if an offence involved a breach of trust; if there was a racist or religious motive behind an offence; or if the victim was particularly vulnerable. They also include any relevant previous convictions held by the *defendant*.

***Agricultural, Horticultural and Forestry Training Board* v *Aylesbury Mushrooms Ltd* (1972)** (*delegated legislation*)**:** an example of procedural *ultra vires*.

■ The training board was required by the *enabling Act* to consult anybody who might be affected by one of its laws. It did not consult the Mushroom Growers' Association and therefore the piece of delegated legislation was void.

aid (*secondary participation*)**:** to give help, support or assistance to the *principal offender*, usually at the scene of the crime.

■ There does not have to be a causative link between the actions of the person providing the aid and the offence committed by the principal offender.

Alcock v Chief Constable of South Yorkshire (1991) (*psychiatric injury — secondary victims*)**:** this case concerns the Hillsborough disaster in 1989 where people were crushed to death at a football match. The 16 *claimants* were friends or relatives of the *primary victims* and suffered psychiatric injury in different ways. Some were at the football ground, some were watching the events unfold live on the television and some had to identify bodies at the mortuary.

■ The *House of Lords* rejected their claims and established the following test for secondary victims:

(1) The psychiatric injury must have been caused by the secondary victim hearing or seeing the accident itself or the immediate aftermath — i.e. the secondary victim must have witnessed the accident with his or her 'unaided senses'. Watching a disaster on television or being told about it by someone else is not sufficient.

(2) The secondary victim must have been present at the event or have witnessed it immediately afterwards. (The definition of 'immediate aftermath' extends to seeing loved ones in hospital, 'so long as he remained in the state produced by the accident up to and including immediate post-accident treatment' (Deane J in *Jaensch v Coffey,* 1984).

(3) The secondary victim must have close ties of love and affection with the primary victim. (The court will assume such a tie between husband and wife and between parent and child. The claimant will be required to prove close ties in cases involving other relatives and friends.)

allurement (*occupiers' liability*)**:** an attraction or temptation.

■ The law accepts that children may be attracted onto *land* or *premises* and the occupier should guard against any kind of allurement that places a child visitor at risk of harm.

■ *e.g. Jolley* v *Sutton LBC (2000).*

alternative dispute resolution (ADR): various methods of resolving civil disputes, without resorting to the formality of a court case.

■ ADR includes *arbitration, mediation, negotiation* and *conciliation. Tribunals* are a popular alternative to the courts.

■ ADR is cheaper than a *civil court* case and its use was promoted by *Lord Woolf* in the *Civil Procedure Rules 1999* in order to reduce the amount of *litigation.*

Anderton v Ryan (1985) (*attempts*)**:** the *defendant* bought a video recorder that she believed to be stolen. After she confessed this to the police, they found no evidence to show that the equipment had actually been stolen but the defendant was nonetheless charged with attempting to handle stolen goods. She was convicted, but on appeal the *House of Lords* quashed her conviction, despite the fact that she was clearly guilty according to the wording of s.1(2) of the *Criminal Attempts Act 1981.*

■ *TIP* This case was overruled a year later by the House of Lords using the *Practice Statement 1966* in *R* v *Shivpuri (1986).*

Animals Act 1971: replaced the *common law* rules relating to liability for animals.

■ As well as distinguishing between dangerous species (*ferae naturae*) and non-dangerous species (*mansuetae naturae*) of animal, the Animals Act 1971 also provides liability for damage done by *trespassing livestock, liability for injury to livestock caused by dogs* and damage caused by *animals straying onto the highway*.

■ A *keeper* is not liable under s.2(2) if he or she is unaware of the animal's characteristic that is likely to cause damage.

■ Defences available for claims made under s.2 are contained in s.5 of the Act:

(1) A person is not liable under sections 2–4 of this Act for any damage which is due wholly to the fault of the person suffering it.

(2) A person is not liable under s.2 of the Act for any damage suffered by a person who voluntarily accepted the risk thereof.

(3) A person is not liable under s.2 of this Act for any damage caused by an animal kept on any premises or structure to a person trespassing there, if it is proved either:

(a) that the animal was not kept there for the protection of persons or property; or

(b) (if the animal was kept there for the protection of persons or property) that keeping it there for that purpose was not unreasonable.

■ *Contributory negligence* may also be a defence under s.10 of the Act. The claimant's *damages* would be reduced accordingly.

animals straying onto the highway: damage caused by animals straying onto the highway can be claimed under s.8 of the *Animals Act 1971* only if a *duty of care* is owed. The normal rules of *negligence* apply.

antisocial behaviour order (ASBO): a civil order made by the *Magistrates' Court* under s.1 of the Crime and Disorder Act 1998.

■ A local authority or chief constable can apply for an ASBO for anyone over the age of 10 who has acted in a manner that caused, or was likely to cause, alarm or distress to a person.

■ Conditions of the ASBO can include a *curfew*, excluding the *defendant* from certain places and preventing him or her from coming into contact with certain people.

■ Breach of the ASBO is a criminal offence.

appellant: a person who appeals to a higher court for the reversal of a decision.

appellate: concerned with appeals.

■ *e.g.* the *Court of Appeal* and *House of Lords* are both appellate courts. They hear appeals from people who want the decision of a lower court to be reversed.

■ Other courts may hear certain appeals, e.g. the divisional courts of the *High Court* and the *Crown Court* can hear specific appeals from the *Magistrates' Court*.

■ See *civil courts routes of appeal* and *criminal courts routes of appeal*.

appropriation (*theft*)**:** defined in s.3(1) of the *Theft Act 1968*:

Any assumption by a person of the rights of an owner amounts to appropriation, and this includes, where he has come by the property (innocently or not) without stealing it, any later assumption of a right to it by keeping or dealing with it as owner.

■ Section 3(2) provides a defence to people who buy stolen goods in good faith:
Where property or a right or interest in property is or purports to be transferred for value to a person acting in good faith, no later assumption by him of rights which he believed himself to be acquiring shall, by reason of any defect in the transferor's title, amount to theft of the property.

■ Appropriation includes assuming any rights of the owner, e.g. touching, moving, selling destroying etc. (see *R v Morris, 1983*).

■ An appropriation can take place even with the *consent* of the victim (see *Lawrence v Metropolitan Police Commissioner, 1972*).

arbitration: a type of *alternative dispute resolution* where a trained arbitrator makes a binding decision.

■ As the parties agree to have their dispute decided by an independent arbitrator, the procedure is less formal than *litigation*. The *small claims track* is a form of arbitration used in the *County Court*, where the *judge* decides the dispute in a less formal way than in a court case. Many businesses include an arbitration clause (known as a *Scott v Avery clause*) in their contracts, which requires both parties to use arbitration should a dispute arise. The Advisory, Conciliation and Arbitration Service (ACAS) uses this method to solve employment disputes, and the Association of British Travel Agents (ABTA) uses arbitration to deal with complaints made by holidaymakers.

■ The Arbitration Act 1996 states: 'The object of arbitration is to obtain the fair resolution of dispute by an impartial tribunal without unnecessary delay or expense.'

arrest: a suspected criminal is taken into custody by the police.

■ The powers of arrest under the *Police and Criminal Evidence Act 1984* have been amended by the Serious Organised Crime and Police Act 2005. Code G has been issued, which gives guidance on the exercise of the powers of arrest. It states that two tests must be met before an arrest can be said to be lawful:
(a) The person must be involved or suspected of involvement or attempted involvement in a crime.
(b) There must be reasonable grounds for believing that the arrest is necessary.

■ The police can arrest anyone who is about to commit an offence or who is committing an offence; anyone the officer has reasonable grounds for suspecting is about to commit an offence; anyone who is reasonably suspected of being guilty of an offence that the officer has reasonable grounds for suspecting has been committed; or anyone guilty of an offence that has been committed.

■ The powers of arrest, which apply to any offence, are subject to the necessity test — the officer must believe that it is necessary to arrest that person. Reasons why an arrest might be necessary are set out in s.2 of Code G and include the need to ascertain the name of the person involved or his or her address, prevent the person causing injury to him- or herself or others, or prevent the person causing damage to property.

■ At the time of arrest or as soon as possible afterwards, the arresting officer is required to record the nature and circumstances of the offence leading to the arrest, the reason why arrest was considered necessary, the fact that a caution was given and anything said by the person at the time of arrest. This information will then be recorded in the custody record on arrival at the station.

arson: defined in s.1(3) of the *Criminal Damage Act 1971*: 'An offence committed under this section by destroying or damaging property by fire shall be charged as arson.'

■ There must be some damage or destruction caused by fire. Singed material would be enough to constitute arson, but property blackened by smoke would not.

■ The *defendant* must either intend or be reckless that property will be damaged or destroyed by fire. There is also an offence of aggravated arson, where the defendant intends or is reckless that life may be endangered by fire.

■ The *mens rea* of arson can be formed after the fire has been started. In *R* v *Miller (1983)*, the defendant accidentally set fire to a mattress when he fell asleep and dropped a lit cigarette. He formed the *mens rea* when he awoke and did nothing to extinguish the fire.

■ *TIP* This offence has a maximum sentence of life imprisonment.

Article 234 referral: a provision of the Treaty of Rome allowing any court or *tribunal* to refer a question of *European Union* law to the *European Court of Justice* if it believes 'a decision on that question is necessary to enable it to give a judgement'.

ASBO: see *antisocial behaviour order*.

assault: a *common law* crime defined in the case of *R* v *Venna* (1976) as 'the intentional or reckless causing of an apprehension of immediate unlawful personal violence'.

■ The *actus reus* of assault is any act that makes the victim fear that unlawful force is about to be used against him or her. No force need actually be applied, and actions such as raising a fist, pointing a gun or brandishing a sword will be sufficient. The victim must fear immediate threat of harm, not at some time in the future. The courts have given a wide interpretation of the word 'immediate' (*Smith* v *Chief Superintendent, Woking Police Station*, 1983).

■ There is no assault if it is obvious to the victim that the *defendant* cannot or will not carry out his or her threat of violence. The defendant may make a statement that negates the threat (see *Tuberville* v *Savage, 1669*).

- Words alone can constitute an assault. In *R* v *Wilson* (1955), Lord Goddard stated of the accused: 'He called out "get out the knives", which itself would be an assault.' Silent telephone calls can constitute an assault (see *R* v *Ireland*, *R* v *Burstow, 1997*).
- The *mens rea* of assault is either *intention* or Cunningham *recklessness*. The defendant must have either intended to cause the victim to fear the infliction of immediate and unlawful force, or must have seen the risk that such fear would be created.
- Assault is a *summary offence* with a maximum sentence on conviction of 6 months' imprisonment or a fine (*Criminal Justice Act 1988*).
- *TIP* When assault and *battery* occur at the same time, it is known as *common assault*.

Associated Provincial Picture Houses v Wednesbury (1948): see *Wednesbury unreasonableness*.

attempts: if a *defendant* fully intends to commit a crime but for some reason fails to complete the *actus reus*, the law on attempts is available to ensure that he or she can still be prosecuted.

- If the defendant is found guilty, he or she will usually face the same maximum penalty that applies to the full offence.
- The law on attempts is contained in s.1(1) of the *Criminal Attempts Act 1981*.
- The *mens rea* of attempts is *intention*, e.g. the *mens rea* for attempted *murder* is an intention to kill; however, an intention to cause *grievous bodily harm*, which would be sufficient for a murder conviction, is not sufficient to make the defendant liable for attempted murder.
- See *R* v *Gullefer (1987)*, *R* v *Geddes (1996)* and *R* v *Shivpuri (1986)*.

attendance centre order (*young offender*): sentences a young offender to go to an attendance centre for a specified number of hours, usually on Saturday mornings.

- These centres are run by the police and include activities that focus on discipline, physical training and social skills.

Attorney General: the *government's* principal legal adviser.

- The prime minister chooses a Member of Parliament (who is also a *barrister*) to act as the Attorney General.
- The Attorney General has many powers, including giving permission for certain cases to be prosecuted, e.g. *murder* cases where the victim died more than 3 years after the original incident (see *Law Reform (Year and a Day Rule) Act 1996*), appealing against lenient sentences and referring cases to the *Court of Appeal* (see *Attorney General's Reference*).

Attorney General for Jersey v Holley (2005) (*provocation*)**:** reverted the law of provocation back to the rule established in *DPP* v *Camplin (1978)*.

- The *defendant* was an alcoholic who killed his girlfriend with an axe while drunk. He did not deny the *murder* but sought to rely on the partial defence of provocation The *Privy Council* decided that the reasonable person was an objective standard and the test is whether the defendant showed the powers of self-control to be expected of an ordinary person of the same sex and age. Other characteristics are only relevant to the gravity of the provocation. Thus, since the powers of self-control to be expected of a defendant are now those of the reasonable person, the objective nature of the test has been restored.

■ *TIP* This was confirmed by the *Court of Appeal* in *R v Mohammed (2005); R v James, R v Karimi (2006)*.

Attorney General's Reference: a case involving a point of law is referred to the *Court of Appeal* by the *Attorney General* under s.36 of the Criminal Justice Act 1972.

■ The Attorney General will do this if he or she thinks it is an area of law that needs clarification. The decision of the Court of Appeal will not affect the original outcome of the case but it can create a new *judicial precedent* for future cases.

■ *e.g.* *Attorney General's Reference No. 3 (1994)*.

Attorney General's Reference No. 3 (1994) (*rerum natura* and *transferred malice*)**:** the *defendant* stabbed his pregnant girlfriend in the abdomen. The baby was born prematurely and later died.

■ The question was whether the defendant could be convicted of the *murder* of the child. The *House of Lords* held that the fact that the child had not yet been born at the time of the attack did not prevent a *murder* conviction when it later died. On the facts, however, it was not possible to transfer the malice (the *intention* to cause *grievous bodily harm* to the mother) to make the defendant liable for the murder of the baby. At best, a conviction for *manslaughter* was a possibility.

Attorney General v PYA Quarries (1957) (*public nuisance*)**:** defines a public nuisance as one that 'materially affects the reasonable comfort and convenience of a class of Her Majesty's subjects'.

■ Blasting at a quarry owned by the *defendants* caused noise and dust that affected 30 nearby residents.

automatism: the involuntary performance of actions.

■ In *Bratty v Attorney General for Northern Ireland (1963)*, Lord Denning defined automatism as 'an act which is done by the muscles without any control by the mind'. Examples include a spasm, a reflex action and an act induced by concussion.

■ With the defence of automatism, the *defendant* claims that the *actus reus* was involuntary and argues that therefore he or she should not be convicted of the offence. Since the defendant denies the *actus reus*, automatism may be used as a defence to all crimes, including those classed as *strict liability* offences.

■ There are two types of automatism: *insane automatism* and *non-insane automatism*.

■ Self-induced automatism caused by drink or drugs is dealt with using the defence of *intoxication*.

bail: the release by the police, *Magistrates' Court* or *Crown Court* of a *defendant* held in *custody*, having arranged for him or her to return to the police station or court at a later date.

■ When a person charged with a criminal offence attends the Magistrates' Court for the first time, the issue of bail is considered. If the *magistrates* think it would be better to keep the defendant in *prison* until his or her next hearing, they will *remand* him or her in custody. This is decided by a 'bail application'.

■ Every defendant has the right to bail, although it can be refused if there are substantial grounds to believe the defendant would fail to surrender to custody, commit an offence while on bail, interfere with witnesses or otherwise obstruct justice. Bail will also not be granted if someone is accused of *murder*, attempted murder, *manslaughter*, rape or attempted rape and has a previous conviction for such an offence. The court must specify why the defendant is not granted bail. The penalty for failure to surrender to bail can be a fine of up to £5,000 or imprisonment for up to 12 months.

■ Bail can be conditional or unconditional. Bail conditions could include reporting to the police station every day; living at a certain address; surrendering one's passport; providing surety; being under a *curfew*; or not being permitted to contact others involved in the case, e.g. *witnesses* or the victim. These conditions are contained in s.3 of the Bail Act 1976.

■ The police are allowed to grant 'street bail' at the time of *arrest* for the *accused* to appear at the police station or Magistrates' Court at a later date. They may also impose conditions to the bail under the Criminal Justice and Public Order Act 1994.

***Baker* v *Willoughby* (1970)** (*negligence — damage/novus actus interveniens*): the *claimant* injured his leg in a car accident caused by the *defendant's* negligence. The defendant was made to compensate the claimant for his injuries. The claimant, however, had to have the injured leg amputated when he was shot during an armed robbery (new act). The defendant claimed that he should no longer have to compensate the claimant for an injury to a leg that no longer existed. The court decided that it was fair for the claimant to receive compensation.

■ *TIP* This decision was not followed in *Jobling* v *Associated Dairies* (1982), where the *House of Lords* held in favour of an employer whose *employee* had been injured at work but then suffered an unrelated illness (new act) that prevented him from working again. The employer was only liable for the injury until the claimant became ill.

balance of probabilities: the civil standard of proof.

■ This standard is lower than the one required for criminal cases, which is '*beyond reasonable doubt*'.

■ *TIP* Although this is the standard of proof in civil cases, it is often used in criminal defences, e.g. *diminished responsibility* need only be established on a balance of probabilities.

Bar Council: the governing body for *barristers*.

■ The Bar Council represents the interests of the Bar and oversees the training and qualification of barristers.

■ A client who is unhappy with the service provided by his or her barrister can complain to the Bar Council. The Complaints Commissioner will investigate any complaints and may refer them to the Professional Conduct and Complaints Committee for its opinion. The Bar Council can then order the barrister to repay fees, suspend the barrister or even disbar the barrister so that he or she can no longer practise.

Barnett v Chelsea and Kensington Hospital Management Committee (1968) (*negligence — damage*)**:** three night watchmen became sick from drinking tea. The hospital they attended telephoned a doctor and described the symptoms. The doctor did not recognise that they had arsenic poisoning and told them to go home. Evidence showed that the doctor did not cause their deaths by not examining them, as they would have died anyway.

■ *TIP* This is an example of the '*but-for*' test of *factual causation*.

barrister: a legal practitioner admitted to plead at the Bar.

■ Barristers are usually self-employed but share administrative costs by working together in *chambers*. A few are sole practitioners and some are employed by various companies and organisations. They are governed and supervised by the *Bar Council*.

■ They specialise in one or two areas of law and are mainly involved in *advocacy*. They wear a wig and gown when they appear in court.

Bar Vocational Course (BVC): the qualification taken after a degree to train to be a *barrister*.

■ The course (which lasts 1 year full time or 2 years part time) covers skills such as case preparation, criminal and civil *litigation*, *advocacy*, opinion writing, ethics and evidence.

basic intent: a crime where *recklessness* or *negligence* will be sufficient to establish the *mens rea*.

■ Examples of basic intent crimes include *involuntary manslaughter*, s.20 *grievous bodily harm*, s.47 *actual bodily harm*, *assault* and *battery*.

b

■ *Involuntary intoxication* provides a defence to basic intent crimes.

battered women's syndrome: a psychological condition resulting from a prolonged period of physical and emotional abuse by a partner. It may be considered an *abnormality of mind* and allow the defence of *diminished responsibility* for a charge of *murder*.

■ See *R v Thornton (No. 1) (1992)* and *R v Ahluwalia (1992)*.

battery: a *common law* offence that involves the intentional or reckless application of unlawful *force* on another.

■ The *actus reus* of battery consists of the application of unlawful force on another. Any unlawful physical contact can amount to a battery: there is no need to prove harm or pain, and a mere touch can be sufficient. Battery can be direct or indirect. Direct battery is force applied directly by one person to another, e.g. a slap or a punch. Indirect force can be applied using an implement or vehicle (see *Fagan v Metropolitan Police Commissioner, 1969*).

■ To constitute a battery, the victim need not be aware that he or she is about to be struck. Therefore, if someone is struck from behind and does not see it coming, this still constitutes a battery. Force does not have to be applied to the person's body. Touching his or her clothing may be enough, even if the victim feels nothing at all as a result (*R v Thomas*, 1985).

■ A battery may be caused by an *omission*. In *R v Santana-Bermudez* (2003), the *defendant* omitted to give warning that he had a hypodermic needle in his pocket during a police search. A police woman was stuck by the needle, which caused bleeding. This was held to constitute a battery.

■ The *mens rea* of battery is *intention* or Cunningham *recklessness*, i.e. intention or recklessness as to the application of unlawful force.

■ Section 39 of the *Criminal Justice Act 1988* provides that battery is a *summary offence*, punishable by up to 6 months' imprisonment or a *fine*.

■ *TIP* When *assault* and battery occur at the same time, it is known as *common assault*.

belonging to another (*theft*): defined in s.5(1) of the *Theft Act 1968* as 'Property shall be regarded as belonging to any person having possession or control over it, or having any proprietary right or interest.'

■ 'Proprietary right or interest' means ownership. The *defendant* must be charged with the theft of the property from the actual owner (see *R v Dyke and Munro, 2002*). Property is still owned even if it has been lost and the owner is no longer trying to find it.

■ Ownerless property cannot be stolen. The courts are keen to ensure that the property has been completely abandoned before they allow it to be regarded as ownerless (see *R v Small, 1988*).

■ A person may be guilty when stealing his or her own property (see *R v Turner (No. 2), 1971*).

bench: the *judge* or *magistrates* presiding over a case.

■ This also refers to the place where the judge or magistrate sits in the courtroom.

b

beneficiary: the person who benefits from a *will*.

beyond reasonable doubt: the standard of proof required in criminal cases.
■ The court must be sure that the *defendant* is to blame.

bill: the name given to an idea for a new *Act of Parliament* as it starts its journey through the *legislation* process at the *parliamentary stage*.
■ There are three types of bill: *public bills, private bills* and *private members' bills*.

binding precedent: the part of a judgement made in a previous case that other *judges* have to follow.
■ The *ratio decidendi* made by a judge high enough in the *hierarchy of the courts* will bind the future decisions of other judges.
■ When a case involves a point of law, the *lawyers* for both parties will research past cases in *law reports*, the internet, journals etc. to find out what decisions have already been made. By doing this, the lawyers can try to speculate the outcome of their own case if the facts are similar to a previous case.
■ *TIP* A past decision is binding only if the case was heard in an appropriate court in the hierarchy and the facts of the new case are sufficiently similar.

bind over: see *breach of the peace*.

***Bolam v Friern Hospital Management Committee* (1957)** (*negligence — breach of duty*): a doctor is expected to reach the standard required of a person at his or her level in the profession. He or she would not be expected to reach the standard of a specialist when he or she is only a junior doctor. Instead, he or she would need to reach the standard of the ordinary reasonable junior doctor.
■ When the court has to decide whether a doctor has been negligent, it will hear evidence from other doctors about their thoughts on what is appropriate practice. The case involved a patient being injured after having electric shock treatment without a relaxant. The court decided that this was not negligent as some doctors did use a relaxant drug while others did not.

***Bolton v Stone* (1951):** (*negligence — breach of duty*) there is no breach of duty when the likelihood of a risk of damage is small.
■ During a cricket match, a batsman hit a ball that struck and injured the *claimant*, who was standing outside the cricket ground. This was a rare occurrence and the cricket club had built a high fence to try to prevent this from happening. The court decided that the *defendants* were not negligent, as the likelihood of the risk was low and people cannot be expected to prevent all accidents (e.g. *Latimer v AEC Ltd, 1952*).

***Bourhill v Young* (1943)** (*negligence — duty of care* and *nervous shock*): it was not foreseeable that a woman would suffer a miscarriage after hearing a motorbike accident. The *defendant* did not owe a duty of care to the *claimant*.

***Bratty v Attorney General for Northern Ireland* (1963)** (*insanity*): the *defendant* strangled his victim during an epileptic seizure. This was treated as a plea of insanity by the courts. The *House of Lords* held that any mental disorder that is prone to recur should be classed as a '*disease of the mind*'.

b

breach of contract: when the terms of a *contract* are not carried out, done badly or done only in part.

■ The other party to the contract can sue for *damages*, rescind (end) the contract or force the party who breached the contract to carry it out properly (specific performance).

breach of duty (*negligence*): the fault element of negligence.

■ The *defendant* must have committed an act or *omission* that fell below the *standard of care* expected in the circumstances. It is established using the *objective test*, e.g. the ordinary reasonable driver in *Nettleship* v *Weston (1971)*.

■ This general standard of care does not require the defendant to prevent harm to others in every conceivable situation (*Bradford-Smart* v *West Sussex County Council*, 2002).

■ When using the objective test, the court takes certain things into account, e.g. the defendant's age (see *Mullin* v *Richards, 1998*) and profession (see *Bolam* v *Friern Hospital Management Committee, 1957*), the characteristics of the *claimant* (see *Paris* v *Stepney Borough Council, 1951*), and how dangerous the situation is (see *Bolton* v *Stone, 1951*).

■ *TIP* The standard of care expected can vary in different cases.

breach of the peace: behaviour that causes or is likely to cause a public disturbance.

■ A person who has breached the peace may be bound over by the court to keep the peace for a certain amount of time.

brief: a summary of the facts and legal points of a case that is given to a *barrister* to argue in court.

■ This word is also used informally to describe a *solicitor* or barrister.

building (*burglary*): discussed in s.9(4) of the *Theft Act 1968*:

> References in subsections (1) and (2) above to a building...shall also apply to an inhabited vehicle or vessel, and shall apply to any such vehicle or vessel at times when the person having a habitation in it is not there as well as at times when he is.

■ In *Stevens* v *Gourley* (1859), Judge Byles defined a building as 'a structure of considerable size and intended to be permanent of at least endure for a considerable time'. A container with wheels is not classed as a building (*Norfolk Constabulary* v *Seeking and Gould*, 1986), whereas a container with the wheels removed is classed as a building (*B and S* v *Leathley*, 1979).

■ The type of building that is burgled affects the length of sentence that the *defendant* will receive. Burglary of a dwelling (a residential building) carries a maximum sentence of 14 years' imprisonment, whereas the burglary of a non-dwelling carries a maximum sentence of 10 years' imprisonment.

■ *TIP* Although the definition in s.9(4) tells us that vehicles and vessels are included, it does not define the word 'building'.

building (part of a) (*burglary*): in *R* v *Walkington* (1979), the *defendant* went into a department store. He went behind the till to look in an open cash register. When he saw that there was nothing in it he closed the drawer. The defendant was charged with burglary under s.9(1)(a). His conviction was upheld, as the *Court of Appeal* believed that what constitutes 'part of a building' is a question of fact for the *jury* to decide.

***Bulmer* v *Bollinger* (1974):** Lord Denning was concerned that membership of the *European Union* would slowly erode all of the UK's *sovereignty* of *Parliament*.

■ Lord Denning famously stated: 'The Treaty is like an incoming tide. It flows into the estuaries and up the rivers. It cannot be held back.'

burglary: defined in the *Theft Act 1968*; according to s.9(1), a person is guilty of burglary if:

(a) he or she enters any building or part of a building as a trespasser and with intent to commit any such offence as mentioned in s.9(2) (stealing, inflicting grievous bodily harm or causing criminal damage)

or

(b) having entered any building or part of a building as a trespasser, he or she steals or attempts to steal anything in the building or that part of it or inflicts or attempts to inflict on any person therein any grievous bodily harm

■ Sections 9(1)(a) and 9(1)(b) cover different situations. Section 9(1)(a) involves entering *premises* with intent to commit one of the *ulterior offences* mentioned in s.9(2). This type of burglary is committed at the time of *entry*. Section 9(1)(b) is the same as s.9(1)(a) but requires that the *defendant* actually carries out the *actus reus* of either *grievous bodily harm*, attempted grievous bodily harm, *theft* or attempted theft. He or she need not have the *mens rea* for the offence at the time of entry.

■ 'Entry' is defined in the cases of *R* v *Collins (1973)*, *R* v *Brown (1985)* and *R* v *Ryan (1996)*. 'Building' is discussed in s.9(4) of the *Theft Act 1968*.

■ *TIP* Section 9(2) also included rape as an ulterior offence, but this was removed by the Sexual Offences Act 2003.

but-for test: see *factual causation*.

Butler Committee and the Criminal Law Revision Committee: criticism of the defence of *insanity*.

■ The Butler Committee suggested that the M'Naghten rules (see *R* v *M'Naghten, 1843*) should be abolished and a new defence introduced. This should apply to *defendants* with a mental disorder and should result in a verdict of 'not guilty on evidence of a mental disorder'. This would avoid the defendant being labelled insane.

■ Others suggest that there is no need for such a defence and that those suffering from insanity should be dealt with outside the criminal justice system.

■ Currently, the burden of proof is on the defence to prove insanity. It has been suggested by both the Butler Committee and the Criminal Law Revision Committee that the burden of proof should be reversed and placed on the *prosecution*.

BVC: see *Bar Vocational Course*.

bylaw: a law made by local councils and other public bodies.

■ Bylaws are a type of *delegated legislation*. All bylaws are checked by the relevant *government* minister to make sure they have not gone beyond the power given to them by *Parliament*.

■ Local councils are given powers to make laws for their area, e.g. to ban the drinking of alcohol in the town centre or to *fine* people who let their dogs foul in public parks.

■ Public corporations such as the buses and train services are able to impose fines for non-payment of fares.

cab-rank rule: self-employed *barristers* are obliged to take the next case that is offered to them.

■ This rule ensures that everyone is able to get legal representation, as barristers should not refuse to take a case when they have the time and skills and are offered a reasonable fee.

CALSA: see *Courts and Legal Services Act 1990*.

***Caparo Industries PLC v Dickman* (1990)** (*negligence — pure economic loss*): the *defendants* were accountants who undertook an annual audit of a company that they worked for. They produced an audit report that made the company look as though it was doing much better than it was. The *claimants* read the audit report and, relying on the favourable information it contained, bought shares in the company. When the claimants lost money on their shares, they sued the defendants. The accountants were not liable for the claimants' losses as they did not have actual knowledge of who would rely on the advice and how they would rely on it.

■ The *special relationship* (required by the *Hedley Byrne and Co. Ltd v Heller and Partners (1964)* test for *negligent misstatement*) is sometimes referred to as an 'assumption of responsibility'. If the court believes that the defendant assumed responsibility, then there will be a special relationship. There was no special relationship in this case.

■ This case also established the three-part test for proving a *duty of care* exists:
(1) Was the *damage* reasonably foreseeable?
(2) Was there sufficient *proximity* between the claimant and the defendant?
(3) Is it just, fair and reasonable to impose a duty of care?

causation: the requirement that the *defendant's actus reus* was the cause of the harm.

■ There are two types of causation: *factual causation* and *legal causation*.

■ *TIP* Causation can also be necessary in civil law, e.g. *negligence* (see *damage*).

caution (*arrest*): the warning given by the police when arresting a suspect.

■ The person must be informed by the arresting officers of the fact of his or her arrest and the reason for it — even if this is obvious. He or she must be cautioned in the following way: 'You do not have to say anything. But it may harm your defence if you do not mention when questioned something which you later rely on in court. Anything you do say may be given in evidence.'

certiorari: an order quashing an *ultra vires* decision.

CFA: see *conditional fee agreement*.

chain of causation: see *legal causation*.

chambers: the offices occupied by a *barrister* or group of barristers.

■ Once *pupillage* is completed, the barrister needs to become a permanent member of a chambers (a 'tenant'). Barristers work together in a set of chambers and share administrative staff known as barristers' clerks.

■ *TIP* Tenancy is notoriously difficult to find and barristers often have to spend time as a 'squatter' in the chambers where they did their pupillage before moving on elsewhere.

Chancery Division (of the *High Court*)**:** deals with *equity* and trusts, taxation, *wills* and other money-related matters.

children (*occupiers' liability*)**:** section 2(3)(a) of the *Occupiers' Liability Act 1957* states that an *occupier* 'must be prepared for children to be less careful than adults'.

■ An occupier's duty towards children is thus to make the *premises* reasonably safe for a child of that age, particularly if there is an *allurement* on the *land*.

■ *e.g.* See *Glasgow Corporation* v *Taylor (1922)*.

circuit judge: hears both criminal and civil cases in the *Crown Courts* and *County Courts*.

■ Circuit judges are assigned to a particular circuit and may sit at any of the Crown Courts and County Courts on that circuit.

■ They are appointed by the queen, on the recommendation of the *Lord Chancellor*.

■ Applicants must have a 10-year Crown Court or 10-year County Court qualification, or have been the holder of one of a number of other judicial offices for at least 3 years.

civil courts: deal with cases involving disputes between individuals (see also *civil courts routes of appeal*).

■ A *claimant* will sue the *defendant* in order to seek a *remedy*.

■ The civil courts include the *House of Lords, Court of Appeal, High Court* and *County Court*. The *Magistrates' Court* also deals with some civil cases.

■ *e.g.* A person involved in a car accident may seek compensation from the driver who caused the accident.

civil courts routes of appeal: the process of taking a case to a higher court in the hope of getting a different decision.

■ The *House of Lords* is the highest appeal court in England and Wales. It only hears appeals with leave (permission granted by the *Court of Appeal* or the House of Lords) on a point of law of general public importance. A *leapfrog appeal* may be made from the *High Court* to the *House of Lords* if the Court of Appeal is already bound by one of its previous decisions (see *judicial precedent*).

C

■ The Court of Appeal hears appeals regarding any civil matter from both the *County Court* and the High Court. It deals with appeals about the facts of the case and points of law raised in the case.

■ The three divisions of the High Court are known as the divisional courts when they hear appeals. The *Queen's Bench Division* deals with appeals from *tribunals,* the Chancery can hear an appeal involving *land* and bankruptcy from the County Court, and the *Family Division* hears appeals from family proceedings in the *Magistrates' Court.*

civil law: the area of law dealing with disputes between individuals (see also *civil courts, contract law* and *tort*).

■ A *claimant* may sue the *defendant* for a *remedy.*

civil liberties: a person's rights and freedoms (see also *Human Rights Act 1998*).

Civil Procedure Rules 1999 (CPR): *Lord Woolf's* reforms of the *civil courts.*

■ His main reforms included:

   (1) greater promotion of *alternative dispute resolution*

   (2) pre-action protocols that encourage the exchange of documents and evidence before the trial

   (3) *judges* to be much more involved in case management, including strict timetabling of cases to reduce delays and setting time limits for how long a trial will run; this allows the parties involved to get a better idea of how much the case will cost

   (4) shared Civil Procedure Rules between the *County Court* and the *High Court*

   (5) the *three-track system* (*small claims track, fast track* and *multi-track*)

civil service: the people who work for *government* departments.

claimant: a person making a claim in a civil case.

CLS: see *Community Legal Service.*

co-accused: more than one person is charged with committing the same crime.

■ If only one person commits a crime, he or she is known as the *principal offender.* If two or more people are co-accused of the same crime, they are known as joint principals.

Code A: see *stop and search.*

Code C: see *police safeguards.*

Code G: see *arrest.*

Codes of Conduct: see *police safeguards.*

coincidence: see *contemporaneity.*

Coke's definition of murder: the classic definition of *murder* given by Sir Edward Coke in his work *Institutes of the Laws of England,* published in 1797:

   Murder is when a man of sound memory, and of the age of discretion, unlawfully killeth within any county of the realm any reasonable creature in *rerum natura* under the King's peace, with malice aforethought, either expressed by the party or implied by law, so as the party wounded or hurt die of the wound or hurt, within a year and a day after the same.

C

Commission (of the European Union): an institution of the *European Union* with both executive and legislative functions.
- The commissioners are 'independent beyond doubt'. They work for the good of the European Union rather than for their individual *member states*. They each have an area of responsibility, e.g. transport or the environment.
- The Commission has two main roles:
  - initiator of new laws — the Commission proposes new laws that the commissioners and their staff consider would be for the benefit of the European Union.
  - guardian of the treaties — the Commission is responsible for making sure that European Union laws are enforced in the member states. If it finds a member state that is in breach of its European Union obligations, it will settle the case in the *European Court of Justice*, e.g. *Tachographs: EC Commission v UK* (1979).

***Commissioners of Customs and Excise v Cure and Deeley* (1962):** an example of substantive *ultra vires* (*delegated legislation*).
- The Finance (No. 2) Act (1940) did not allow Customs and Excise to charge extra for late tax returns, so when they started to fine people they were challenged in the courts. The *judge* found that they had acted beyond their power and therefore the demand for extra money was void.

Committal for sentence: the procedure whereby someone convicted in the *Magistrates' Court* is sent to the *Crown Court* for *sentencing*.
- *Indictable offences* do not need to be committed to the Crown Court. They are sent there directly under s.51 of the Crime and Disorder Act 1998.
- If the case is an *either-way offence*, the Magistrates' Court will hold committal proceedings, which include a summary of the facts and law by the prosecution. This is a paper-based hearing (no witnesses need to attend) and is governed by rule 7 of the Magistrates' Courts Rules 1981. At the end of the hearing the *magistrates* decide if there is sufficient evidence to commit the case to the Crown Court. This test is set out in s.6(1) of the Magistrates' Courts Act 1980.

committee stage (of the *parliamentary stage* of the *legislation* process)**:** where a *bill* is scrutinised by a group of MPs called the *standing committee*.
- These committees are usually composed of between 16 and 30 MPs, reflecting the composition of *Parliament*. Any suggestions made at the *second reading* are considered and the committee may propose amendments, additions and deletions to the bill. This is followed by the *report stage*.

common assault: when the offences of *assault* and *battery* occur at the same time.

common law: law made by *judges*.
- There are some areas of both *criminal law* and *civil law* that have not been codified by *Parliament*.

- **e.g.** *Murder* (in criminal law) and *negligence* (in civil law) are both common law offences.

Common Professional Examination (CPE): see *Graduate Diploma in Law (GDL)*, the new name for the CPE.

- This is commonly known as a 'law conversion course'. If undertaken full time, it is a year-long course that covers the same foundation subjects as a law degree.

Community Legal Service (CLS) (*legal aid*)**:** an organisation that is in charge of administering civil advice and assistance.

- The most common matters that people seek assistance for are debt, asylum, housing, employment, community care and education. The assistance received differs according to the type of problem, but ranges from advice to taking cases to court.

- Only those firms of *solicitors* with a contract with the CLS can carry out publicly funded work. To get a contract, the solicitors' firm needs to have a 'Quality Mark', which is awarded only after inspection by the CLS.

- **TIP** The 'Quality Mark' can also be awarded to other advice providers such as Citizens Advice Bureaux, law centres and community organisations.

community sentence: a punishment or *rehabilitation* scheme that is an alternative to a *custodial sentence*.

- Anyone aged 16 or over can be given a community sentence and it is seen as more effective at rehabilitating offenders than sending them to *prison*. Under s.148 of the Criminal Justice Act 2003, it can be passed only if the offence is serious enough to warrant it.

- A community punishment order (formerly known as 'community service') may include between 40 and 300 hours of unpaid work in the community, such as cleaning graffiti or collecting charity bag donations. *Young offenders* who are aged 16 or 17 are given a specified number of between 40 and 240 hours.

- A community rehabilitation order includes supervision by the *Probation Service*; treatment for drug or alcohol addiction; or anger, alcohol or drug training programmes that look at an offender's behaviour. Such an order can be imposed on young offenders who are aged 16 or 17 and is known as a *supervision order*.

- A *curfew* may require an offender to remain in a specified place at certain times.

community service: now called a community punishment order.

- See *community sentence*.

compensatory damages: money that is awarded to put a person back in the position he or she was in before a *tort* was committed.

- **e.g.** If a motorist has negligently caused £1,000 worth of damage to your car, compensatory damages would award you that amount.

- This is the most common *remedy* sought in a civil case. When calculating the amount of compensation, the *judge* will consider general *damages* (also known

as *non-pecuniary losses*) for injury and losses where it is difficult to give an exact price, e.g. pain and suffering (*Hicks* v *South Yorkshire Police,* 1992), and loss of amenity (*West and Son* v *Shephard,* 1964). There are tariff guidelines issued by the *Court of Appeal* for the amount of compensation that a person suffering from different injuries can claim, but the amount of compensation awarded will vary with different circumstances.

■ If the *claimant* can no longer work, his or her loss of earnings is calculated using the *multiplicand* (the amount that the court thinks the claimant's earnings would have altered, e.g. through promotion or changing job) and the *multiplier* (a calculation of the amount of money required to invest that will give the annual income to which the claimant is entitled). It follows that multiplicand × multiplier = loss of earnings compensation.

■ The court will also consider special damages (often known as *pecuniary losses*), including loss of earnings up to the date of the trial, medical expenses, damage to *property* and any other loss that the claimant may have incurred.

conciliation: a type of *alternative dispute resolution.*

■ A conciliator discusses the dispute with the parties and encourages them to find a solution upon which they both agree. Most disputes involving employment try this method before the case goes to an employment *tribunal.* The Advisory, Conciliation and Arbitration Service (ACAS) offers this service to encourage an employer and *employee* to come to an agreement.

conditional fee agreement (CFA): a written agreement made between a *solicitor* and a client, where it is usually agreed that the client will not have to pay the solicitor's costs if he or she loses the case.

■ Following the Access to Justice Act 1999, some cases that previously qualified for *legal aid* were no longer eligible for public funding, e.g. personal injury cases.

■ Often advertised under the slogan 'No win, no fee', CFAs were introduced by the *Courts and Legal Services Act 1990.*

■ The client may still have to pay the costs of the other side and other expenses relating to the case, and he or she should be advised to take out insurance to cover these. If the client wins, he or she pays the solicitor's fee plus an added percentage — sometimes known as an *'uplift fee'.* This is to compensate the solicitor for taking the risk of non-payment. Usually, the higher the risk of losing, the higher the uplift fee, but such fees are capped at twice the usual fee.

■ *TIP* Since the Access to Justice Act 1999, solicitors' costs, including the uplift fee, are recoverable from the losing party.

conduct crime: an offence where the *actus reus* is prohibited conduct.

■ *e.g. Perjury* is a conduct crime, where the *defendant* is guilty if he or she lies under oath in court, even if the lie has no effect on the outcome of the case, for example if the *judge* or *jury* does not believe him or her.

consent: agreement of the victim to minor harm inflicted on him or her may prevent the *defendant* from incurring liability for what would otherwise be an offence.

■ Consent operates as a defence because the courts recognise that individuals have autonomy over their own lives. However, there are limits as to what a person may consent to, and while consent may be available as a defence to non-fatal and sexual offences (see *R v Slingsby, 1995*), it is not available for charges of *murder* or *manslaughter*, as no one may consent to his or her own death at the hands of another (see *Pretty v UK, 2002*).

■ The victim's consent to the harm will be valid only if he or she understands the nature of the act and knows exactly to what he or she is consenting (see *R v Richardson, 1998*). The victim must have the capacity to consent — children and those suffering from mental illness are not able to give valid consent (see *Gillick v West Norfolk and Wisbech AHA, 1986*).

■ A victim may consent to *assault* or *battery*. In *Collins and Wilcock* (1984), it was stated that people are also taken to consent impliedly to the 'physical contacts of ordinary life'. However, certain activities inevitably mean that the victim will sustain injury beyond assault or battery, e.g. surgery, tattooing and piercing, and sports.

■ *TIP* For consent as a defence in civil cases, see *volenti non fit injuria*.

consideration: the third requirement of a valid *contract*.

■ After acceptance, a contract requires that there is an exchange by both parties of something of value. This can be money, goods, services or a promise. The exchange between the parties does not need to be of equal value.

■ Exchanges that take place before a contract is accepted are known as *past consideration* and will not be allowed. Consideration that takes the form of something illegal or something that one of the parties is already under a duty to do also will not be enforced by the courts.

consolidation fund: the money from which *judges* are paid their salary.

■ Judicial salaries are not voted for by *Parliament*. This helps to promote *judicial independence* and ensures that wages cannot be used as a bargaining tool.

conspiracy (*inchoate offences*)**:** an agreement between two or more persons to embark on a course of conduct that, if carried out as planned, would amount to an offence.

■ Conspiracy is defined in the Criminal Law Act 1977.

■ *TIP* Conspiracy is an inchoate offence, which means that the full crime was not committed.

constructive manslaughter (*involuntary manslaughter*)**:** an offence that requires the *defendant* to have committed an unlawful and dangerous act.

■ The act must be unlawful and cause the victim's death. The normal rules of *causation* apply. The case of *R v Franklin* (1883) stated that the unlawful act must also be a criminal offence rather than a *tort* (*civil law*). There have been many drugs cases that have required the courts to assess what an unlawful act is (see *R* v *Kennedy, 1999*). Other unlawful acts include *assault* (see *R* v *Mitchell, 1983*), *arson* (*R* v *Goodfellow*, 1986) and *criminal damage* (*R* v *Newbury and Jones*, 1976).

■ The unlawful act must be considered dangerous. The test for dangerousness was established in *R* v *Church (1967)*. It is an *objective test* in that the '*ordinary reasonable man*' would see a risk of some harm.

■ The unlawful act cannot be an *omission* (*R* v *Lowe*, 1973).

■ The *mens rea* is the one required to commit the unlawful and dangerous act. The defendant does not have to intend or foresee death (see *R* v *Lamb, 1967*). The *transferred malice* rule applies to constructive manslaughter (see *R* v *Mitchell, 1983*).

consultation stage: the second stage of the *legislation* process where the idea for a new law is discussed with experts and interested parties.

■ A *Green Paper* is formulated. This is known as a 'discussion document'. The finalised version of the idea is then produced as a *White Paper*, which is the *government's* 'statement of intent'.

consumer protection: laws that protect people who buy goods and services.

■ *e.g.* The Consumer Protection Act 1987 enforces *strict liability* on the producer, supplier or importer of a defective product that has caused personal injury or *damage* to *property*.

■ *e.g.* The Sale of Goods Act 1979 provides that goods bought from a business must be of 'satisfactory quality' (s.14), the seller must be the legal owner of the goods he or she is selling (s.12) and the goods must match their description (s.13).

contemporaneity: the *actus reus* and *mens rea* must coincide.

■ In situations where the *actus reus* comes first, the courts apply the 'continuing act' doctrine, where the *actus reus* is stretched over time to meet the point where the defendant had *mens rea*.

■ In other cases, it may be that the *mens rea* comes first. In this situation, the courts apply the 'one transaction' doctrine (established in the case of *R* v *Fagan*, 1969 and confirmed by the *House of Lords* in *R* v *Miller, 1983*). This can occur when the defendant hits the victim and knocks him or her unconscious. The defendant might assume that the victim is dead rather than unconscious and then try to dispose of the body. The victim is then actually killed during the disposal process (as occurred in *Thabo Meli* v *R*, 1954).

contemptuous damages: the amount of money awarded in a civil case may be decreased to show disapproval of a *claimant's* decision to take a case to court in the first place.

■ *e.g.* In *Pamplin* v *Express Newspapers Ltd* (1988), the claimant sued the *Daily Express* for *defamation* when it called him 'sleazy'. Pamplin had avoided paying parking tickets by registering his car in the name of his infant son. Although the court found in favour of Pamplin, the *judge* awarded him only the lowest coin of the realm, which in 1988 was half a pence.

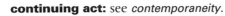

C

continuing act: see *contemporaneity*.

contract: a legally binding agreement that is enforceable in the courts.

■ A contract requires an *offer, acceptance* and *consideration*. There also needs to be *intention to create legal relations* and the people involved must have the capacity to form a valid contract.

■ Preliminary negotiations of a contract are known as an *invitation to treat* (see *Fisher* v *Bell, 1961*).

contractual duty to act (*omission*)**:** there may be a duty to act for someone whose job it is to do so.

■ *e.g.* A lifeguard is under a duty to help someone who is drowning and may be criminally responsible for any injuries suffered by the victim if he or she fails to act.

■ In *R* v *Pittwood* (1902), the *defendant* was a gatekeeper at a level crossing. One day, he left the gate open and went for lunch. A hay-cart attempting to cross the line was hit by a train, and the driver was killed. The defendant was convicted of manslaughter. His conviction was based on his failure to perform his contractual duty, i.e. to shut the gate when the train was approaching.

contributory negligence: a *claimant's* carelessness for his or her own safety or interests which contributes to damages that he or she sustains.

■ *e.g.* A car passenger who fails to wear a seatbelt may suffer more serious injuries in a car accident.

■ The *defendant* must be proved to be *negligent* and then the claimant's amount of *damages* will be reduced according to the percentage to which he or she was to blame for his or her injuries. An example is a claimant who would have been awarded £10,000 in damages but who is found to have been 50% contributorily negligent. The claimant would then receive £5,000 damages rather than the full £10,000.

■ The relevant statute in this area is the Law Reform (Contributory Negligence) Act 1945. Section 1(1) states:

> Where any person suffers damage as the result partly of his own fault and partly of the fault of any other person or persons…the damages recoverable…shall be reduced to such extent as the court thinks just and equitable having regard to the claimant's share in the responsibility for the damage.

The reduction depends on the facts in each case, but the courts have laid down guidelines for cases of road accidents in which the claimant was not wearing a seatbelt (see *Froom* v *Butcher, 1976*).

■ *TIP* Allowances are made most notably for children, e.g. *Evans* v *Souls Garage* (2000).

control test (*vicarious liability*)**:** a test maintaining that if the employer is in control of the way that a person's work is carried out, this may establish that the person is an *employee*.

■ This test was used in many early cases. However, if the work is especially skilled or sophisticated, the test becomes less effective.

- **e.g.** Surgeons are employed by NHS trusts. These trusts are run by managers who do not have the relevant knowledge to instruct the surgeons on how to carry out operations. Despite this, surgeons are considered to be employees.

conveyancing: the preparation of documents for the buying and selling of *property*.

- Before 1985, *solicitors* had a monopoly on conveyancing. Nowadays, people in other professions can train to become licensed conveyancers.

cooling-off period *(provocation)*: a time gap between the *provocative conduct* and the *defendant* killing the victim.

- There should be no cooling-off period as this gives the defendant time to think about his or her actions.
- The longer the delay and the more evidence of deliberation, the more likely it is that the attack will be viewed as one of revenge rather than provocation.
- See *R v Ibrams and Gregory (1981)*.

Corcoran v Anderton (1980) *(robbery)*: one of the *defendants* hit the victim across the back while the other pulled at her handbag. The victim screamed as the handbag fell to the ground and the defendants ran off empty handed. The defendants were found guilty of robbery. The *appropriation* occurred when the defendant grabbed the bag. It did not matter that the bag was then dropped, as he had assumed at least one of the rights of the owner when he grabbed it. The *theft* was complete and therefore the charge was one of robbery rather than attempted robbery.

coroners' court: court involved in the investigation of suspicious and sudden deaths and the allocation of treasure trove.

- The coroner is medically or legally qualified.
- A *jury* makes a decision in cases involving death in prison and police *custody*, to see if there was any *negligence* on the part of the police or prison service. A jury was also used to decide whether the police were responsible for the deaths of those who died during the Hillsborough disaster in 1989.
- If a person discovers treasure, the coroner's court decides whether he or she can keep it or whether it must be given to a museum.

Council of Ministers: the 'effective centre of power' of the *European Union* that decides which of the *Commission's* proposals should be made into law.

- The council includes one minister from each *member state*. The ministers change according to the issue that is being discussed, e.g. for farming matters, the minister for rural affairs will attend. For important issues, the prime minister will attend.
- The council has the final say on the majority of proposals from the Commission. Members may vote by simple majority, unanimously or by *qualified majority voting*.

counsel: the *barrister* conducting a case.

counsel *(secondary participation)*: to encourage the *principal offender* before the crime is committed.

■ This may include advising the principal offender or supplying him or her with information or equipment.

■ There does not have to be a causative link between the actions of the counsellor and the offence committed by the principal offender.

counter-offer: a response to an *offer* that seeks to introduce different terms.

■ *e.g.* In *Hyde* v *Wrench* (1840), the offer to sell a farm for £1,000 was rejected when Hyde made a counter-offer of £950. The counter-offer was rejected and Hyde tried to accept the original offer of £1,000. He was not able to do this as the counter-offer had extinguished the original offer.

County Court: a court that hears the majority of civil cases.

■ County Courts are local courts and there are approximately 300 of them across England and Wales.

■ They deal with most *divorce* cases and cases that are worth less than £15,000 (less than £50,000 for personal injury cases).

■ The *Small Claims Court* is part of the County Court and deals with cases worth less than £5,000. This court uses a less formal procedure (*arbitration*) to decide liability. The parties in such a case are encouraged to represent themselves and avoid the cost of hiring a *solicitor*.

course of employment (*vicarious liability*)**:** an employer is only liable for *torts* that an *employee* commits while doing his or her job.

■ The classic test is that of Salmond, taken from the text *Salmond on Torts*, which stated that tortious acts are done in the course of employment if they are wrongful acts actually authorised by the employer; or wrongful and unauthorised ways of doing acts authorised by the employer. Thus, the employer will be vicariously liable for the employee's tort when:
  • the employee does an authorised act in a careless way
  • the employer has allowed the employee to do an unlawful act
  • the employee carries out an authorised act in an unauthorised way
  • the employee carries out an act that has been expressly forbidden but is for the benefit of the employer

■ See *Limpus* v *London General Omnibus Co. (1862)*, *Lister* v *Hesley Hall (2001)* and *Rose* v *Plenty (1976)*.

court clerk: see *legal adviser*.

Court of Appeal: court that hears appeals from the *High Court* and *Crown Court*.

■ See *criminal courts routes of appeal* and *civil courts routes of appeal*.

Court of Appeal judge: decides cases in the *Court of Appeal*.

■ Court of Appeal judges are known as Lord and Lady Justices of Appeal.

■ They are appointed by the queen on the recommendation of the prime minister, who has been advised by the *Lord Chancellor*. The Lord Chancellor will have consulted senior members of the *judiciary*.

■ The statutory qualification is a 10-year *High Court* qualification or being a *High Court judge*.

■ *TIP* Most Court of Appeal judges are promoted from the ranks of experienced High Court judges.

Courts and Legal Services Act 1990 (CALSA): legislation that made major changes to the legal profession.

■ *Solicitors* no longer have exclusive rights over the conduct of *litigation*, as *barristers* can be approached directly in some circumstances.

■ Solicitors can now gain higher rights of audience, as barristers have lost their exclusive right to *advocacy* in the higher courts.

■ The Act created the *Legal Services Ombudsman*.

CPE: see *Common Professional Examination*.

CPR: see *Civil Procedure Rules 1999*.

CPS: see *Crown Prosecution Service*.

creator of a dangerous situation (*omission*)**:** if someone creates a risk of harm to another's person or *property*, he or she is under a duty to act in order to prevent the harm or at least limit the harm caused. If he or she does not do so, he or she may be liable for any resulting consequences (see *R* v *Miller, 1983*).

Criminal Attempts Act 1981: statute defining the law on *attempts*.

■ Section 1(1) states:

> If with intent to commit an offence to which this section applies, a person does an act which is more than merely preparatory to the commission of the offence, he is guilty of attempting to commit the offence.

■ Section 1(2) states:

> A person may be guilty of attempting to commit an offence to which this section applies even though the facts are such that the commission of the offence is impossible.

Criminal Case Review Commission: established following the *Runciman Commission* report to consider cases where a possible miscarriage of justice has occurred.

■ The commission can suggest cases to the *Court of Appeal* that have previously not been granted an appeal.

criminal courts: courts that deal with cases involving activities punishable by the state.

■ The prosecution tries to prove *beyond reasonable doubt* that the *defendant* is guilty. If he or she is found guilty, the *judge* will impose a sentence. All criminal cases start at the *Magistrates' Court*. A *jury* at the *Crown Court* hears the more serious cases.

■ Appeals can be made to the *Court of Appeal* and the *House of Lords* (see *criminal courts routes of appeal*).

criminal courts routes of appeal: taking a case to a higher court in the hope of getting a different decision.

■ The *House of Lords* only hears appeals with leave (permission granted by the *Court of Appeal* or the House of Lords) on a point of law of general public importance.

■ The prosecution may appeal to the criminal division of the Court of Appeal if it believes a *defendant* has received a lenient sentence or has been wrongly acquitted, so that the law is changed for the future. Permission to appeal is known as 'with leave', and this is granted by the *Crown Court* or the Court of Appeal. The defence may appeal if it believes the sentence was too harsh (without permission), or against conviction either on a point of law or fact (with permission). An appeal regarding the facts of the case requires new evidence before it will be allowed. The *Criminal Case Review Commission* may recommend that the Court of Appeal allow an appeal in a case where it believes a miscarriage of justice has occurred. The Court of Appeal can dismiss the appeal, vary a sentence, order a retrial or quash the conviction.

■ A case decided in the *Magistrates' Court* may be appealed to the Crown Court, where a *circuit judge* and two *magistrates* will retry a case in which the defendant believes that he or she was wrongly convicted (based on the facts of the case) or that the sentence was too harsh. The Crown Court does not hear appeals concerning a point of law. These are appealed from the Magistrates' Court to the *Queen's Bench Division* of the *High Court.*

criminal damage: offence defined in s.1(1) of the *Criminal Damage Act 1971* as:

> A person who without lawful excuse destroys or damages any property belonging to another intending to destroy or damage or being reckless as to whether property is being destroyed or damaged commits an offence.

■ There are four elements to the *actus reus*:

(1) Destroys or damages:

- The amount of *damage* needs to be sufficient. In *A (a juvenile)* v *R* (1978), spitting on a policeman's coat was not sufficient to constitute criminal damage as it could be easily wiped off.
- The damage should affect the value or usefulness of the *property*. In *Morphitis* v *Salmon* (1990), a scratch to a scaffolding pole did not constitute criminal damage.
- It is considered that damage has been caused when the property requires cleaning that has to be paid for. In *Hardman* v *Chief Constable of Avon and Somerset Constabulary* (1986), the *defendant* drew a picture on the pavement with chalk. This was regarded as criminal damage as the council had to pay to have it cleaned off. The damage does not have to be permanent.

(2) Property: defined in s.10(1) of the Criminal Damage Act 1971 as 'property of a tangible nature whether real or personal including money'.

- The definition of property for criminal damage is different from that for *theft*. It includes *land* (which theft does not), but it does not include *intangible property* such as shares (which is included in theft).

(3) *Belonging to another:* this is similar to the crime of theft yet the Criminal Damage Act 1971 uses the words 'custody or control', whereas the *Theft Act 1968* uses the word 'possession'.

- Section 10(2) of the Criminal Damage Act 1971 defines 'belonging to another' as '…where the other has custody or control of it; or has a proprietary right or interest in it; or has charge of it'.

(4) Without lawful excuse: section 5 of the Criminal Damage Act 1971 gives examples of actions that would constitute a lawful excuse and thus a defence to criminal damage charges.

- Section 5(2)(a) covers the situation where the defendant believes that the owner would have consented to the damage (*R* v *Denton*, 1982).
- Section 5(2)(b) allows damage to occur when the defendant believes other property was in immediate need of protection (*R* v *Hill and Hall*, 1988).
- Section 5(3) provides that the defendant's 'belief' required in s.5(2)(a) and s.5(2)(b) is honestly held (*Jaggard* v *Dickinson*, 1980).

■ The defences defined in s.5(2)(a) and s.5(2)(b) have always been regarded as subjective (based on what the defendant honestly believed). The courts have since added an objective element into s.5(2)(b). It is up to the *jury/magistrates* to decide if they believe that the defendant acted to prevent damage to property (not that the defendants themselves thought so). This was established in *R* v *Jones* (2004), where the defendants damaged a military base in the hope that it would prevent an attack on Iraq.

■ *TIP* These defences apply to criminal damage, *aggravated criminal damage* and *arson*.

■ The *mens rea* of criminal damage is either *intention* to destroy or damage property or *recklessness*. Recklessness is defined using a *subjective test* established in *R* v *Cunningham (1957)*. See *R* v *G and Another (2003)*.

Criminal Damage Act 1971: statute defining the crimes of *criminal damage*, *aggravated criminal damage* and *arson*.

Criminal Defence Service: an organisation set up by the *Legal Services Commission* to administer criminal *legal aid*.

■ *Solicitors* and others who wish to carry out work funded by the Criminal Defence Service must apply for a contract and are checked regularly to make sure that they are providing high-quality work at a reasonable cost.

■ *TIP* The aim is to ensure that people suspected or accused of criminal offences receive a fair hearing and are able to respond properly to the allegations against them. It is a requirement of the *Human Rights Act 1998* that people receive a fair trial, and an inability to afford legal assistance would obviously jeopardise this.

Criminal Justice Act 1988 (*assault* and *battery*): section 39 provides that assault and battery are *summary offences* with a maximum sentence on conviction of 6 months' imprisonment or a *fine*.

criminal law: the area of law dealing with offences committed against the state (e.g. *murder*, *theft* etc.).

■ A person charged with a criminal offence will be prosecuted by the *Crown Prosecution Service* and, if found guilty, will be sentenced. Compare *civil law*.

Criminal Law Act 1967: section 3(1) defines *self-defence* as:

> A person may use such force as is reasonable in the circumstances in the prevention of crime, or in effecting or assisting in the lawful arrest of offenders or suspected offenders or of persons unlawfully at large.

Criminal Procedure Act 1991 (*insanity*)**:** statute establishing a variety of court orders available to a *defendant* who is not guilty by reason of insanity.

■ Before this Act was passed, a *judge* had to order the defendant to stay for an indefinite period in a mental institution. This meant that many people were reluctant to raise the defence of insanity and preferred, instead, to serve a prison sentence.

■ Since this Act was passed, a judge can make a hospital order, a guardianship order, a supervision and treatment order or an absolute discharge for crimes other than *murder*.

cross-examine: to question the opposition's *witnesses*.

■ *e.g.* In a criminal case, the prosecution will call its witnesses and question them. They will then be cross-examined by the defence.

Crown Court: the main criminal trial court that deals with serious cases.

■ The Crown Court tries *indictable offences*, and *either-way offences* if the *defendant* has requested that his or her trial be held there. If the defendant pleads guilty, the *judge* alone will pass sentence. If the defendant pleads not guilty, a *jury* will try the case and, if it finds the defendant guilty, the judge will impose a sentence.

■ The Crown Court also hears appeals from the Magistrates' Courts.

Crown Prosecution Service (CPS): the *government* organisation responsible for prosecuting those charged with a criminal offence.

■ The CPS was created under the Prosecution of Offences Act 1985. Prior to this, the police used to investigate and prosecute criminal cases.

■ The CPS works both in offices and in police stations, reviewing cases submitted to it and deciding who to charge and who to release. If a person is to be charged, the CPS decides what he or she will be charged with.

■ Decisions on whether to prosecute are based on a two-stage test in the Code for Crown Prosecutors. The CPS first considers whether the evidence available gives a realistic prospect of conviction in court and, if so, it must then consider whether it is in the public interest to prosecute. It will take into account the circumstances of the offence, looking at the motive behind it and how it was carried out, e.g. if a weapon was used or whether the victim was serving the public. If both tests are satisfied, a prosecution will go ahead.

cumulative provocation (*provocation*)**:** previous acts or words may be taken into account when considering whether the *defendant* was provoked.

■ This idea of 'slow-burn provocation' has been used in domestic violence cases, where women who have suffered years of abuse at the hands of their partners finally 'snap' and kill them. Since they would usually have to wait for an

opportunity to attack their partners, provocation was traditionally denied to them as they failed the 'sudden and temporary' loss of control requirement.
- See *R v Thornton (No. 1) (1992)* and *R v Ahluwalia (1992)*.

curfew: a *community sentence* requiring an offender to remain in a specified place at certain times.
- The court determines the hours between which the offender must stay in his or her house.
- A penalty is imposed for breach of a curfew order. The curfew is usually monitored by fitting an electronic tagging device to the offender's ankle.

custodial sentence: sending an offender to prison.
- In criminal law, the most severe sanction for those over the age of 21 is imprisonment. Under the Criminal Justice Act 2003, the court can pass a custodial sentence only if it thinks that the offence was so serious that neither a *fine* alone nor a *community sentence* can be justified for it. It may also be imposed to protect the public from violent or sex offenders.
- Some offences have a mandatory sentence, e.g. the only sentence that can be passed for *murder* is life imprisonment. The Powers of Criminal Courts (Sentencing) Act 2000 also lays down minimum sentences for some crimes, e.g. drug trafficking offences and *burglary*.
- It is rare for a prisoner to serve his or her full sentence. Usually, those sentenced to less than 4 years will be released after serving half of their sentence. Those with a longer sentence will have to serve two-thirds of their sentence before release. When they are released, offenders remain on licence for the remainder of their sentence. Those sentenced to life may apply for *parole* once they have served the recommended tariff, but if released, they will remain on licence for life.
- A *suspended sentence* defers a custodial sentence for 6 months to 2 years. The offender will not go to prison unless he or she commits another offence within that time.

custody: imprisonment.
- A suspect may be held in custody to return to court at a later date for another hearing or the trial.
- Every *defendant* has the right to *bail,* with some exceptions.
- A defendant may be found guilty and awarded a *custodial sentence* by the *judge* or *magistrate.*

damage (*negligence*): loss or harm; the final element required to prove negligence.

■ There must be some sort of damage for a negligence case to succeed, e.g. personal injury or damage to *property*.

■ The *breach of duty* must have caused the damage. This is established using the *but-for test*: would the *claimant* have suffered damage regardless of the *defendant's* act or *omission*? (See *Barnett* v *Chelsea and Kensington Hospital Management Committee, 1968*.) In some cases it can be difficult to establish what caused the claimant's damage. *Wilsher* v *Essex Area Health Authority* (1988) involved multiple causes. *Fairchild* v *Glenhaven Funeral Services* (2002) allowed a claim even though *causation* could not be established. This is referred to as the 'Fairchild exception'.

■ The claimant must prove that the type of damage suffered was reasonably foreseeable. It is not enough to prove that any damage is foreseeable; it must be proved that the particular type of damage suffered is foreseeable. This was established in the case of *Wagon Mound (1961)*. Also see *Smith* v *Leech Brain and Co. Ltd (1962)*.

■ Sometimes a new intervening act will break the *chain of causation* (*novus actus interveniens*).

damage (*private nuisance*): the second requirement of private nuisance.

■ Discomfort or inconvenience is sufficient for a claim in nuisance: there is no need for physical damage to have occurred. However, a claim involving physical damage is much more likely to succeed and may allow a claim that would otherwise fail (*St Helens Smelting Co. Ltd* v *Tipping, 1865*).

damages: money awarded in a civil case.

■ The most common type of damages is *compensatory damages*. However, the court may award *contemptuous damages, aggravated damages* or *exemplary damages*.

DCA: see *Department for Constitutional Affairs*.

defamation: a false statement about a person that tends to lower his or her reputation in the opinion of right-minded people.

■ Slander means that the false statement is made by spoken words or gestures. Libel means that the false statement is made in permanent form (writing, pictures, film, television or radio broadcasts, or posted on the internet). Libel is usually actionable in *tort*, but it can also be a criminal offence

■ Defamation cases usually involve newspapers that have printed false statements. Such cases are heard in the *High Court*.

defect of reason (*insanity*)**:** the *defendant's* ability to reason is impaired.

■ This term comes from the rules formulated in the case of *R* v *M'Naghten (1843)*.

■ A defendant who still possesses powers of reason but fails to use them cannot be classed as insane.

■ In *R* v *Clarke* (1972), the defendant was charged with *theft* after taking items from a supermarket without paying for them. She claimed that she was suffering from depression that had caused her to be absent-minded and she did not remember putting the items in her bag. She was denying the *mens rea* element of the defence, but the trial *judge* ruled that this amounted to a plea of insanity. In order to avoid indefinite detention in a hospital, she then pleaded guilty. On appeal her conviction was overturned. The court accepted that she still possessed powers of reasoning; it was just that she had failed to use them in this instance.

defendant: a person on trial for a criminal offence or being sued in a civil case.

delegated legislation: laws made by councils and other organisations with the permission of *Parliament*.

■ Parliament does not have the time or expertise to pass every law that is needed each year. It therefore gives some of its power to other people and organisations to make laws. It gives this power through an enabling Act, also known as a parent act.

■ Types of delegated legislation are *bylaws, statutory instruments* and *Orders in Council*.

de minimis rule: see *legal causation*.

denunciation: 'naming and shaming' an offender in order to punish him or her for a criminal offence.

■ If the offender is made known to the public, society is able to express its disapproval at the behaviour of the individual and condemn it.

■ *e.g.* In the USA, convicted shoplifters are sometimes made to stand outside the shop that they stole from with a sign proclaiming they are thieves.

■ *TIP* There is a debate currently taking place about the naming of paedophiles. A media campaign was launched to try to change *government* policy after the murder of Sarah Payne by a child sex offender in 2000. However, this campaign was unsuccessful.

Department for Constitutional Affairs (DCA): a *government* department responsible for the provision of *legal aid*.

■ This department replaced the *Lord Chancellor's* department as it was felt that the Lord Chancellor's role was incompatible with the theory of the *separation of powers*.

detention: depriving a person of his or her freedom against his or her will following *arrest*. The police have the power to hold a suspect in *custody*.

■ The custody officer will assess the strength of the evidence against the suspect and decide whether the suspect can be charged.

■ If there is not enough evidence to charge the suspect at that stage, he or she will be detained so that the police have time to gather the necessary evidence. Often, police will try to obtain the required evidence by interviewing the suspect. The suspect has a right to have someone informed of his or her detention and to be told where he or she is being held. This can be delayed if the detention relates to an *indictable offence* and the delay is considered necessary to protect evidence or prevent harm to others.

■ The custody officer will review whether there is enough evidence to charge after the first 6 hours. Further reviews will be carried out every 9 hours. Generally, the police can detain suspects for up to 36 hours, timed from their arrival at the station. This may be extended for a further 12 hours by the police themselves, but it must be done by an officer of superintendent rank or above. A further and final extension of up to 96 hours is permitted, but this must be approved by a *magistrate*.

■ The interview is tape-recorded and the suspect has the right to consult a legal adviser.

deterrent: a punishment aimed at discouraging an offender from repeating his or her offences or deterring others from committing similar offences.

■ A specific deterrent applies to an individual and the aim is to deter that particular person from reoffending.

■ A severe punishment for a crime may act as a general deterrent to the public. This is often used to try to reduce the number of specific crimes being committed.

Dicey: a nineteenth-century author who wrote *Law of the Constitution* and created the *rule of law*.

diminished responsibility: a partial defence to *murder* that reduces the charge to *voluntary manslaughter*. It is defined in s.2 of the *Homicide Act 1957*.

■ The *defendant* must have:

    (1) *abnormality of mind* (see *R* v *Byrne, 1960*), arising from a condition of arrested or retarded development of mind (i.e. mental deficiencies) or *inherent causes* (see *R* v *Dietschmann, 2003*), or *induced by disease or injury* (see *R* v *Tandy, 1989*).

    (2) substantial impairment (*R* v *Seers*, 1984)

■ The defendant must prove, on the *balance of probabilities*, that he or she was suffering from diminished responsibility at the time of the killing. Medical evidence will be required from at least two experts to substantiate any such claim.

■ *TIP* If the defendant raises diminished responsibility as a possible defence, the prosecution is able to put to the *jury* the alternative defence of *insanity*.

direct effect: the ability of a citizen to rely on a *European Union* law in his or her country's courts.

■ *Treaties* have a horizontal direct effect (a citizen can rely on the treaty against other individuals, such as his or her employer) and a vertical direct effect (a citizen can rely on the treaty against his or her *government*).

direct intention: the state of mind of a *defendant* who sets out to achieve a particular result or consequence.

■ This is sometimes explained by saying that the defendant foresaw a particular result as a certainty and wanted to bring it about.

■ It was defined in *R* v *Moloney (1985)* as 'a true desire to bring about the consequences'.

■ *e.g.* The defendant shoots his or her victim in the chest because the defendant wants to kill him or her.

directive: a type of *European Union* law.

■ Directives are not directly applicable. They require the *member state* to change its law to produce a certain result, but they allow the member state to decide exactly how to do that. The European Union imposes a time limit by which the directive must be implemented. A citizen or a member state can rely on a directive in their national courts if the state has failed to meet the time limit or implement the directive properly. This means that directives have a vertical *direct effect* (established by the *European Court of Justice* in the case of *Van Duyn* v *Home Office*, 1974).

Director of Public Prosecutions (DPP): the head of the *Crown Prosecution Service*.

discharge: the release of a convicted *defendant* without imposing a punishment.

■ A conditional discharge means that the offender will have a criminal record but no further action will be taken against him or her, as long as he or she does not commit a further offence within a specified time period of up to 3 years. If the offender does commit a further offence, he or she may be re-sentenced for the original offence as well as receiving the sentence that is passed for the second offence.

■ An absolute discharge means that the offender will have a criminal record but no further action is taken against him or her.

discharge of a contract: the termination of a contractual obligation.

■ A *contract* may come to an end when it is completed, frustrated (no longer possible to carry out), it has been breached by one of the parties or a new agreement has been made.

disclosure: sharing evidence in a criminal or civil case.

■ In a civil case, both parties should disclose all their evidence according to the *Civil Procedure Rules 1999*.

■ In a criminal case, the prosecution must disclose any evidence that suggests the *defendant* may be not guilty. The defence must provide the prosecution with a written statement of the main elements of the defence.

■ The disclosure of evidence is important to try to avoid miscarriages of justice.

■ *TIP* In the case of the Birmingham Six, where the defendants were wrongly convicted, the police failed to disclose evidence that pointed to their innocence.

disease of the mind (*insanity*)**:** a broad term used in the definition of insanity to include both mental and physical conditions.

■ This term comes from the rules formulated in the case of *R v M'Naghten (1843).*

■ Examples of conditions that have been considered a 'disease of the mind' include arteriosclerosis (hardening of the arteries) in the case of *R v Kemp* (1957), epilepsy in the case of *R v Sullivan* (1984), hyperglycaemic diabetes in the case of *R v Hennessy* (1989), and sleepwalking in the case of *R v Burgess* (1991).

■ The *House of Lords* held that any mental disorder that is prone to recur should be classed as a disease of the mind.

dishonesty (*theft*)**:** an element of liability in theft.

■ The *Theft Act 1968* does not define the word *mens rea*, but it does give some guidance in s.2(1) as to what would not be considered dishonest. According to this section, a person's appropriation of property belonging to another is not to be regarded as dishonest if he or she appropriates the property in the belief that:

  ● he or she has in law the right to deprive the other of it, on behalf of himself or herself or a third person (e.g. you took something you thought was yours)

  ● he or she would have the other's consent if the other knew of the appropriation and the circumstances of it (e.g. you borrowed something you thought the owner would let you borrow)

  ● the person to whom the property belongs cannot be discovered by taking reasonable steps (e.g. you found 10 pence in the street)

■ *TIP* The *Court of Appeal* established a two-stage test for dishonesty in *R v Ghosh (1982).*

distinguish (*judicial precedent*)**:** to avoid following a *binding precedent* when the material facts of a new case are significantly different.

■ *e.g.* In *R v Wilson (1996)*, the *Court of Appeal* distinguished from the *House of Lords'* decision in *R v Brown and Others (1993).*

district judge: a judge who hears cases in the *County Court*, District Registries of the *High Court* or *Magistrates' Court.*

■ *e.g.* District judges (Magistrates' Court) are paid and deal with the full range of cases. They usually hear the longest and most complicated cases.

■ They are appointed by the *Lord Chancellor*. Applicants require a 7-year general qualification.

divorce: a court order that terminates a marriage.

■ According to the Matrimonial Causes Act 1973, the only ground for divorce is an irretrievable breakdown of marriage.

■ Divorce is a two-stage process. The first stage is the granting of a decree nisi; 6 weeks later, the petitioner may apply for a decree absolute.

■ Couples who are seeking a divorce are encouraged to attend *mediation* sessions in order to settle any financial and childcare issues as amicably as possible without going to court (Family Law Act 1996).

doli incapax: Latin for 'incapable of doing wrong'.

■ A child under the age of 10 cannot be found responsible for a crime that he or she commits.

Donoghue v Stevenson (1932) (*negligence*)**:** established who owes a *duty of care* according to the *neighbour principle*.

■ Donoghue suffered gastroenteritis after drinking a bottle of ginger beer that contained a dead snail. She sued Stevenson, the manufacturer of the drink. However, the drink had been bought for Donoghue by a friend, and therefore she could not make a claim under *contract law*. The *House of Lords* made a landmark decision when it decided that there was a duty of care, and Donoghue's claim was successful.

■ *TIP* The neighbour principle has since been replaced by the three-stage test from *Caparo Industries PLC v Dickman (1990)*.

DPP: see *Director of Public Prosecutions*.

DPP v Camplin (1978) (*provocation*)**:** the *defendant* was a 15-year-old boy and the victim was a 50-year-old man who had sexually abused him. The man had abused the defendant and then laughed, at which point the defendant hit and killed him with a chapatti-pan. At his trial, the *judge* directed the *jury* to judge the defendant according to the standards of an adult male. The *House of Lords* held that this was incorrect and maintained that the correct direction was to consider the effect that the provocation would have on a reasonable 15-year-old boy. The question was not would the reasonable adult have acted in the same way but whether the reasonable 15-year-old boy would have done so.

■ The reasonable person is taken to be an ordinary person with the same powers of self-control as someone of the same age and sex as the defendant and sharing such characteristics as would affect the gravity of the provocation.

DPP v Majewski (1977) (*intoxication*)**:** the *House of Lords* explained the defence of intoxication by distinguishing between crimes of *specific intent* and crimes of *basic intent*.

■ The *defendant* had been drinking and taking drugs for a number of hours when he became involved in a fight. He was charged with a number of counts of *assault* against members of the public and the police officers who had been trying to *arrest* him. At his trial, he claimed that he could not remember anything of the incident because of the effects of the alcohol and drugs that he had taken. The House of Lords held that *voluntary intoxication* could not provide a defence to crimes of basic intent and he was therefore guilty.

drafting stage: the third stage of the *legislation* process, where the idea for a new law is written into legal terminology.

■ The *Parliamentary Counsel* is a group of legal experts who draft the idea. After it has been drafted, the idea becomes a *bill* and is ready to be presented to *Parliament*.

***Dulieu v White and Sons* (1901)** (*psychiatric injury — primary victim*): the *claimant* was working behind the bar in a public house when a horse and cart crashed into the bar. The claimant was not physically injured, but her claim for psychiatric injury was successful as it was foreseeable that harm could occur.

duration (*private nuisance*): the courts are more likely to consider a *nuisance* as being *unreasonable* if it lasts for a long time or occurs during unsociable hours.

■ *e.g.* In *Crown River Cruises Ltd* v *Kimbolton Fireworks Ltd* (1996), a firework display lasting only 20 minutes was considered a nuisance when sparks set fire to a barge.

duress: pressure, especially actual or threatened physical force, put on a person to commit a criminal offence.

■ There are two types of duress: *duress by circumstances* and *duress by threats*.

■ Duress cannot be used as a defence for *murder* (see *R* v *Howe, 1987*) or attempted murder (*R* v *Gotts,* 1991). However, duress is a complete defence for most crimes.

■ The burden of proof is on the prosecution to disprove that the *defendant* was under duress.

duress by circumstances (*duress*): the *defendant* will have a defence if he or she commits a crime when feeling forced to do so because of the situation that he or she is in.

■ Like *duress by threats*, this type of duress requires a fear of imminent death or serious injury (*R* v *Baker and Wilkins,* 1997).

■ It has mainly been used as a defence for driving offences, where defendants claim to have felt forced to commit a driving offence because of the circumstances that they found themselves in, rather than because they had been threatened to commit an offence (see *R* v *Conway, 1989* and *R* v *Martin, 1989*).

■ The defence has been extended to other crimes, e.g. possession of a firearm in *R* v *Pommell* (1995) and hijacking in *R* v *Abdul-Hussain* (1999).

duress by threats (*duress*): for this defence, the *defendant* has both the *actus reus* and *mens rea* for the crime, but escapes conviction because his or her will is overborne by personal threats or by threats to family members or people for whom the defendant is responsible.

- The ability to use this defence has been reduced since the case of *R* v *Hasan (2005)*.
- The test for this defence is made up of two parts and was established by the *Court of Appeal* in *R* v *Graham (1982)*.

Dutch courage (*intoxication*)**:** courage acquired from drinking alcohol or taking drugs.

- If someone deliberately drinks alcohol or takes drugs to give himself or herself 'Dutch courage' to commit a crime, his or her intoxication cannot be used as a defence for any crime.
- *e.g.* *Attorney General for Northern Ireland* v *Gallagher* (1963).

duty of care (*negligence*)**:** the legal obligation to take reasonable care to avoid causing damage.

- A duty of care is a connection between the *claimant* and the *defendant*. This connection was originally proved using the *neighbour principle* established by Lord Atkin in *Donoghue* v *Stevenson (1932)*. However, *judges* started to make *policy decisions* to avoid certain people owing a duty of care even when they were closely and directly affected.
- The neighbour principle has since been modified into a three-stage test defined in *Caparo Industries PLC* v *Dickman (1990)*.

duty solicitors: *solicitors* who are available either at the police station or at the *Magistrates' Court*; they give free legal advice to those who require their assistance.

duty to retreat (*self defence*)**:** a principle that called into question whether, if faced with the choice, a *defendant* must retreat or if he or she could choose to stay and fight while still relying on self-defence.

- In *R* v *Bird* (1985), the defendant was at a party to celebrate her seventeenth birthday when her ex-boyfriend arrived with his new girlfriend. The defendant and her ex-boyfriend began to argue. He hit her and she retaliated, forgetting that she had a glass in her hand. The glass broke and caused serious injuries to the victim. The trial *judge* said that she could rely on self-defence only if she had shown an unwillingness to fight. The *Court of Appeal* disagreed, and held that there may be situations when the defendant might react immediately without retreating. The matter was for the *jury* to consider. This established that the defendant is not under a duty to retreat and may strike first in self-defence.

ECJ: see *European Court of Justice*.

economic reality test (*vicarious liability*)**:** a test that examines the terms of a *contract* in order to decide whether a person is an *employee*.

■ It may be a contract of service, in which case the person is more likely to be an employee, or it may be a contract for services, which would indicate that the person is an *independent contractor*. (See *Ready Mixed Concrete* v *Minister of Pensions and National Insurance, 1968*.)

eggshell skull rule: see *thin-skull rule*.

either-way offence: an offence that may be tried at the *Magistrates' Court* or at the *Crown Court*, depending on the circumstances or severity of the case.

■ *e.g. Theft* is an either-way offence.

ejusdem generis (Latin term used in *statutory interpretation*)**:** a rule stating that general words that follow specific ones are to be of the same type as the specific ones.

■ *e.g.* In *Beswick* v *Beswick* (1968), the words 'other property' were interpreted by the court to refer to *land* only. This was because the case concerned the Law of Property Act 1925, which related to land law only.

employee (*vicarious liability*)**:** an employer is only responsible for the *torts* committed by persons who are defined as employees, not for those committed by *independent contractors*.

■ in order to establish who is an employee, the courts can use the *control test, integration test,* or the *economic reality test.*

employer's indemnity (*vicarious liability*)**:** under the Civil Liability (Contribution) Act 1978, an employer found vicariously liable may in turn sue its *employee* to recover some or all of the *damages* awarded against it. *Common law* also allows the employer to recover damages from the employee in certain circumstances.

employers' liability: see *vicarious liability*.

enabling Act: see *delegated legislation*.

entry (*burglary*)**:** the definition of entry has changed from the requirement that it is 'substantial and effective' (see *R* v *Collins, 1973*) to just 'effective' (see *R* v *Brown, 1985)*, to the person trying to enter merely having some part of the body inside the *premises,* even if he or she was unable to steal anything (see *R* v *Ryan, 1996*).

equity: a set of legal principles developed by the *Chancery Division* of the *High Court.*

EU: see *European Union.*

European Convention on Human Rights: an international agreement established after the Second World War to protect people's rights and freedoms.

■ The Council of Europe established the convention in 1950 and set up the European Commission for Human Rights to deal with alleged breaches of human rights. Such cases would be resolved in the *European Court of Human Rights.*

■ The UK ratified (signed) the convention in 1951 and then officially incorporated its provisions into UK law with the passing of the *Human Rights Act 1998.*

European Court of Human Rights: court set up by the Council of Europe to decide cases involving human rights that had not been resolved by the European Commission for Human Rights. Based in Strasbourg, the court hears cases involving alleged breaches of human rights and makes decisions according to the *European Convention on Human Rights.*

■ In the UK, a case may be appealed from the *House of Lords* to the European Court of Human Rights, e.g. *Pretty* v *UK (2002).*

■ *TIP* This court is not connected to the *European Union.* The *European Court of Justice* decides European Union matters.

European Court of Justice (ECJ): an institution of the *European Union* consisting of *judges* from each *member state* who decide cases involving Community law.

■ The ECJ is situated in Luxembourg. One judge is appointed from each member state. The judges hold high judicial positions in their home country and are appointed for 6 years. They are assisted by *Advocates General* who research the cases sent to the court and produce written opinions. The ECJ has a judicial role and a supervisory role.

• The judicial role is to decide cases brought against member states or European Union institutions. Proceedings against member states can be brought by other member states or by the *Commission.* The Commission's role as 'guardian of the treaties' allows it to force a member state to abide by European Union law.

• The supervisory role involves cases that are referred to the ECJ by a court in a member state. If a court in the UK is deciding a case that involves European Union law and it is not sure how it should be applied, it can refer the case to the ECJ for a decision (see *Article 234 referral*).

European Parliament: an institution of the *European Union* consisting of Members of the European Parliament (*MEPs*) elected from each *member state.*

■ The European Parliament is able to hold the *Commission* and *Council of Ministers* accountable. It is involved in the law-making process of the European Union by consultation, cooperation or co-decision:

- Consultation is where the European Parliament is asked for its opinion on a draft proposal from the Commission, to help the Council of Ministers decide if it wishes to approve it or not. The Council of Ministers does not have to follow the recommendations made by the European Parliament.
- Cooperation is used for laws that affect the internal market. The European Parliament is consulted and, once the Council of Ministers has approved the proposal, the European Parliament can suggest amendments. The Council of Ministers can ignore these amendments if the ministers vote unanimously.
- Co-decision is used for laws affecting international agreements. The European Parliament can veto these types of proposals if the Council of Ministers refuses to accept its suggestions for amendments.

European Union (EU): an economic community of European countries.

■ The origins of the EU date back to the Treaty of Paris 1951. Six European countries signed the treaty and agreed to pool their coal and steel production. The European Economic Community was established by the Treaty of Rome in 1957.

■ The purpose of the European Economic Community was to prevent future wars, help countries rebuild their economies after the Second World War, and provide economic and social solidarity and stability in the *member states*.

■ The European Economic Community became the European Union on 1 November 1993. Over the years, the EU has grown. It now includes 27 European countries (member states) and makes laws relating to a wide range of issues, including the environment and the rights of workers. The institutions of the EU are the *European Parliament, Commission, Council of Ministers* and *European Court of Justice*.

euthanasia: the act of ending in a painless way the life of someone suffering from a terminal illness or an incurable disease.

■ Euthanasia is illegal in the UK and is classed as *murder*.

■ Voluntary euthanasia is legal in some countries (e.g. the Netherlands) and requires the *consent* of the patient. Involuntary euthanasia is where the patient's life is ended without his or her consent.

■ Currently, a moral debate surrounds this issue. Some people argue that voluntary euthanasia should be legalised in the UK.

exemplary damages: a punitive measure that seeks to punish the unsuccessful party in a civil case by awarding the winner more *damages* than are necessary to compensate him or her.

***ex parte*:** Latin for 'without one party'.

■ Sometimes this is written in a case name to indicate that a case has been brought without one of the parties being involved (e.g. *R* v *Secretary of State for Transport ex parte Factortame, 1990*).

express consent (*volenti non fit injuria*): a verbal or written agreement to take a risk.

expressio unius est exclusio alterius (a Latin term used *in statutory interpretation*): a rule maintaining that when the *Act of Parliament* states a list of specific items, other similar items are not to be included.

■ *e.g.* In *Tempest* v *Kilner* (1846), the Act of Parliament specified 'goods, wares and merchandise'. The specific nature of the wording meant that 'stocks and shares' were not included.

express malice (*murder*): *intention* to kill.

express permission (*occupiers' liability*): a person has express permission if he or she has actively gained permission to be in a place, for example he or she has been invited to enter the premises.

■ Permission can be withdrawn, but the person must be given a reasonable amount of time to leave before he or she becomes a *trespasser*.

express term: a specifically agreed part of a *contract*.

■ *e.g.* Prices and dates are agreed for the delivery of an item.

■ Some terms are implied by the *common law* and by *statute* (*implied terms*).

extrinsic aids (also known as 'external aids'): sources other than an *Act of Parliament* that may aid a *judge* in trying to interpret the law.

■ A judge may use a dictionary, legal textbooks, the *Human Rights Act 1998*, other similar Acts of Parliament or the *common law* that went before, a *Law Commission* or a *Royal Commission* report, the *Interpretation Act 1978*, explanatory notes included with the Act of Parliament and *Hansard*.

ex turpi causa non oritur actio: Latin for 'an action cannot be based on a disreputable cause'; the principle that the courts may refuse to enforce an action arising out of the *claimant's* illegal or immoral conduct.

■ *e.g.* An injured bank robber could not sue his getaway driver for crashing the car.

■ This concept does not apply in criminal law (see *R* v *Wacker, 2002*).

Factortame: see *R* v *Secretary of State for Transport ex parte Factortame (1990).*

factual causation: the question of whether the *defendant's* actions caused the harm as a matter of fact.

■ The test for factual causation is the but-for test — but for the defendant's actions, would the victim have suffered harm? If the answer is no, the defendant is criminally liable. (See *R* v *White, 1910.*)

■ Once the prosecution has proved factual causation, it must then prove *legal causation.*

Fagan v *Metropolitan Police Commissioner* (1969) (*contemporaneity*)**:** while parking his car, the *defendant* accidentally drove over a policeman's foot. He then refused to move and switched off the car's engine. When charged with *assault,* Fagan tried to argue that he did not have the *actus reus* and *mens rea* at the same time. He claimed that the *actus reus* occurred when he drove onto the foot, but he had no *mens rea* at the time, as it was an accident. He later developed an *intention* to remain on the foot but claimed that the *actus reus* was complete by then. The courts did not accept his argument and his appeal was rejected. It was held that driving onto the foot and remaining there was a 'continuing act' and it was enough that Fagan had *mens rea* at some point during it.

false imprisonment: the restriction of a person's liberty or freedom of movement without lawful excuse.

■ This is a *tort* of *strict liability* that often arises in the context of *arrest* by the police or security guards. It is possible to commit this tort without physical imprisonment, since it requires only that the person's liberty be restrained.

■ There must be a total restraint on the person's freedom of movement in every direction. If there is a reasonable escape route available, there is no false imprisonment.

■ This tort could be committed while someone was unconscious or asleep.

■ A person may be lawfully arrested and, if this happens, he or she has no claim for false imprisonment — see *police powers.*

■ *TIP* 'False' in this sense means 'wrongful'.

Family Division (of the *High Court*)**:** deals with *divorce* and other family matters, such as cases involving children.

fast track: trials held at the *County Court* that involve cases worth between £5,000 and £15,000 (between £1,000 and £50,000 for personal injury).

■ A *circuit judge* hears the case. The trial lasts for no more than 1 day and a trial date is set within 30 weeks.

Fatal Accidents Act 1976: a statute conferring the right to recover *damages* for loss of support on dependants of a person killed in an accident.

fault-based liability: a person is held liable only if he or she is proven to be at fault.

■ In criminal law, the prosecution must prove that the *defendant* did the *actus reus* and had the *mens rea*. *Murder* is a fault-based crime. To be liable, the defendant must have committed an unlawful killing (*actus reus*) with the *intention* (*mens rea*) to kill or cause serious harm.

■ Certain *torts* require the *claimant* to prove that the defendant caused the *damage* (i.e. it was his or her fault). *Negligence* is a fault-based tort. The requirement of a *breach of duty* means that the claimant must prove that the defendant was at fault. This can be particularly difficult to prove in cases involving medical negligence, as a doctor will not be at fault if another doctor would have acted the same way in similar circumstances (see *Bolam* v *Friern Hospital Management Committee, 1957*).

ferae naturae: a dangerous species of animal.

■ Defined in s.6(2) of the *Animals Act 1971* as a species:
  (a) not commonly domesticated in the British Isles, and
  (b) whose fully grown animals normally have such characteristics that they are likely, unless restrained, to cause severe damage or that any damage that they may cause is likely to be severe

filibustering: wasting time through false argument.

■ This tactic may be employed by opposition MPs to use up parliamentary time. It is particularly used to waste the 10 minutes given to *private members' bills*.

fine: a financial penalty imposed by the court.

■ *Magistrates* can give a maximum fine of £5,000, but there is no maximum amount set in the *Crown Court*. When setting the level of a fine, the court must take into account not only the seriousness of the offence but also the financial means of the *offender*, as the offender may go to prison if the fine is not paid.

■ *TIP* According to the Home Office, fines are imposed in approximately 71% of cases each year, making them by far the most common type of sentence.

first-degree murder: the *Law Commission* has suggested that *homicide* offences should be defined according to a hierarchy that reflects the seriousness of the various offences. First-degree murder would apply to the *defendant* who intended to kill, or who killed through an *intention* to do serious injury with an awareness of a serious risk of causing death.

- **TIP** The Law Commission proposals also include definitions of *second-degree murder* and *manslaughter*.

first reading (of the *parliamentary stage* of the *legislation process*)**:** where the title of the *bill* is read out by the MP who is sponsoring it.

- The bill is then published and a date is set for the *second reading*.
- **e.g.** The home secretary would sponsor a bill involving the power of the police.

Fisher v Bell (1961): a case example of the *literal rule* of *statutory interpretation*.

- This case concerned a flick knife displayed in a shop window. Literally, this was not an 'offer for sale', which was specified in the *statute*. Lord Parker acquitted Bell under the Restriction of Offensive Weapons Act 1959, even though it was obvious that this was exactly the sort of behaviour that *Parliament* intended to stop. Lord Parker justified his decision because the parliamentary draftsmen knew the legal term 'invitation to treat' but failed to include it, so to respect Parliament's *sovereignty*, he had to infer that they had left it out on purpose.
- **TIP** Parliament later amended the Restriction of Offensive Weapons Act.

follow (of *judicial precedent*)**:** to apply the law of a previous case to a new case with similar material facts.

force (*robbery*)**:** for the offence of robbery, force must be applied or threatened immediately before or at the time of stealing.

- The court has to decide how 'immediate' the threat must be before the stealing and at what point the *theft* is complete.
- In *R* v *Hale* (1978), the *defendants* forced their way into the victim's house. One of the defendants went upstairs and stole a jewellery box, while the other used force to tie up the victim. The *Court of Appeal* upheld their conviction for *robbery*, despite the fact that it was impossible to say whether the theft occurred at the same time as the force. The theft was a *continuing act* and therefore it was still happening when the victim was being tied up.

fraud: the Fraud Act 2006 came into force on 8 November 2006. It abolishes all the deception offences in the Theft Acts (obtaining property by deception, obtaining services by deception and evasion of liability by deception) with three new fraud offences.The maximum sentence for fraud is 10 years.

- Section 2 (fraud by false representation) states:

  An offence will be committed where a person dishonestly makes a false representation, in order to gain for himself or another, or cause or expose another, to loss or risk of loss.

  The *actus reus* requires that the accused made a false representation. The *mens rea* requires that the accused knew that the representation was, or knew that it might be, false and acted dishonestly, and with intent to gain or cause loss.

- Section 3 (fraud by failing to disclose information) states:

  An offence will be committed where a person dishonestly fails to disclose, to another person, information which he is under a legal duty to disclose.

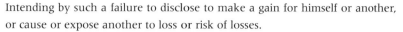

> Intending by such a failure to disclose to make a gain for himself or another, or cause or expose another to loss or risk of losses.

The *actus reus* requires failing to disclose information which he is under a legal duty to disclose. The *mens rea* requires acting dishonestly and an intention to make a gain or cause a loss.

■ Section 4 (fraud by abuse of position) states:

> An offence will be committed where a person, who occupies a position in which he is expected to safeguard the financial interests of another person, dishonestly abuses that position with the intention of gaining something for himself or causing another to lose.

The *actus reus* requires abusing a position of trust. The *mens rea* requires acting dishonestly and an intention by the abuse to make a gain or cause a loss.

■ *TIP* Obtaining services by deception has been replaced by section 11 Fraud Act 2006 and is now defined as *obtaining services dishonestly.*

Froom v Butcher (1976) (*contributory negligence*)**:** the *claimant* was involved in a collision when the *defendant's* car, which was speeding on the wrong side of the road, crashed into his vehicle. The claimant was not wearing a seatbelt and suffered more serious injuries than he would have done had he been wearing the restraint. The *Court of Appeal* laid down set percentages by which damages would be reduced in such cases.

■ If wearing a seatbelt would:
  - not have made any difference to the injuries sustained — no reduction
  - have lessened the severity of the injuries — 15% reduction
  - have prevented the injuries — 25% reduction

frustration: the unforeseen termination of a *contract* as a result of an event that either makes its performance impossible or illegal or prevents its purpose from being achieved.

fusion debate: the legal arguments put forward to 'fuse' *solicitors* and *barristers.*

■ By removing the distinction between solicitors and barristers, these legal professionals would have the same training and *rights of audience* and be known as *lawyers.*

***Gammon Ltd v Attorney General of Hong Kong* (1985)** (*strict liability*)**:** the *defendants* were carrying out building work in Hong Kong when part of the building collapsed because of the builders' failure to follow their original plans. Regulations in Hong Kong made it an offence to change building plans substantially, and the defendants were charged with an offence. They argued that they did not know their deviation was 'substantial'. The *Privy Council* held it was an offence of strict liability and gave guidance on how such decisions were made.

■ The courts presume that *mens rea* is required in criminal cases, particularly if the offence is 'truly criminal'. The *presumption* applies to statutory offences and can be rebutted only if the *statute* states that the offence is one of strict liability or there is a clear implication that this is the case. The presumption can be displaced only when the statute deals with a matter of social concern, and only then if strict liability will assist to prevent it.

Gammon propositions (*strict liability*)**:** in the case of *Gammon v Attorney General of Hong Kong (1985)*, the courts gave guidance as to when a crime would be regarded as one of strict liability.

GBH: see *grievous bodily harm*.

Gillick competence: see *Gillick v West Norfolk and Wisbech AHA (1986)*.

***Gillick v West Norfolk and Wisbech AHA* (1986)** (*consent*)**:** parents may give consent on behalf of their child until the child has sufficient understanding of what is proposed.

■ This is sometimes termed *Gillick competence*.

■ *e.g.* A 14-year-old child may be competent enough to consent to medical treatment without the permission of his or her parents.

***Glasgow Corporation v Taylor* (1922)** (*occupiers' liability*)**:** a 7-year-old child was attracted to some poisonous berries on one of the bushes in the park controlled by the *defendant* corporation. The bush was unfenced and there was no warning notice. The defendants were liable when the child died as a result of eating the berries since they were an *allurement*. The corporation would probably not have been liable if an adult had done the same thing. However, since the berries were particularly attractive to children, and the

g

council was aware that they were poisonous, it should have removed them or secured the area.

golden rule (*statutory interpretation*): when a *judge* alters the interpretation of the words in an *Act of Parliament* in order to avoid an absurdity.

■ This rule is an extension of the *literal rule*.

■ It has both a narrow and a broad approach. The narrow approach is where the judge uses an alternative interpretation of a word to avoid an absurd result (see *R v Allen, 1872*). The broad approach is where a judge does not apply the literal meaning of a word, so as to avoid an absurd result, as in *Re Sigworth* (1935).

government: the political party that has a majority in the *House of Commons*.

■ The leader of that party will become the prime minister.

■ The government is voted into power at a general election.

Graduate Diploma in Law: a qualification that allows non-law students to train to be a *solicitor* or *barrister* after graduating from university.

Green Paper (*legislation*): document produced at the *consultation stage* of the legislation process.

■ This is known as a 'discussion document' and contains a rough draft of the possible things that could be included in the *bill*.

grievous bodily harm (GBH): really serious physical injury.

■ There are two types of GBH, both defined in the *Offences Against the Person Act 1861* s.18 and s.20.

■ The *actus reus* for both sections is unlawfully and maliciously wounding or inflicting GBH. In *DPP v Smith* (1961), the *House of Lords* emphasised that GBH should be given its ordinary meaning, i.e. 'really serious harm'.

■ The difference between GBH in s.18 and s.20 is the *mens rea*. Section 18 GBH is more serious and carries a higher sentence: the *defendant* must have intended to cause really serious harm to be convicted under this section. Section 20 GBH requires only that the defendant intended some harm or was reckless that some harm would be caused.

■ In *R v Dica (2004)*, the *Court of Appeal* held that a person could be liable for s.20 GBH by infecting another person with AIDS.

■ To satisfy the *mens rea* the prosecution must prove intention, i.e. intention to cause GBH or an intention to avoid *arrest*.

■ *TIP* The crucial difference between s.20 and s.18 GBH is in the *mens rea*: while *recklessness* can be sufficient for s.20, intention is always required for s.18.

Griffiths v Lindsay (1998) (*negligence — duty of care*): the court decided that it was not fair for a taxi driver to owe a duty of care to a drunk passenger who got run over as he got out of the vehicle.

gross negligence manslaughter (*involuntary manslaughter*): offence defined in the case of *R v Adomako (1995)*. It requires a *duty of care*, a *breach of duty* that caused death, and a risk of death:

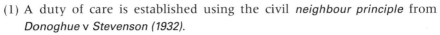

(1) A duty of care is established using the civil *neighbour principle* from *Donoghue* v *Stevenson (1932)*.

- It is a question of law as to whether the *defendant* owes a duty of care and therefore it is an issue for the *judge* to decide (see *R* v *Wacker, 2002*).
- The courts have been reluctant to establish a duty of care in certain circumstances, e.g. a man did not owe a duty of care to his friend whom he left to sleep in a car and who later died (*Lewin* v *CPS*, 2002).

(2) Breach of duty, means that the defendant has fallen below the *standard of care* expected of the '*ordinary reasonable man*'.

- The breach must be serious. It is up to the *jury* to 'consider whether the extent to which the defendant's conduct departed from the proper standard of care incumbent upon him, involving as it must have done a risk of death to the victim, was such as it should be judged criminal' (Lord MacKay in *R* v *Adomako, 1995*).
- The breach of duty must have caused death. This means that the rules of *causation* must also be proved.
- In *R* v *Becker* (2000), a doctor whose patient died from an overdose of the painkillers that he had prescribed was not guilty of gross negligence manslaughter, as he had not fallen below the standard of care expected of the ordinary reasonable doctor.

(3) In *R* v *Singh* (1999), the trial judge directed the jury that: 'The circumstances must be such that a reasonably prudent person would have foreseen a serious and obvious risk not merely of injury or even serious injury but of death.' This suggests that the 'risk of death' requirement of gross negligence manslaughter is now regarded as an *objective test*.

■ The *mens rea* of this crime is described as gross negligence. Lord Mackay in *R* v *Adomako (1995)* quoted Lord Heward (*R* v *Bateman*, 1925) in an attempt to define the *mens rea* of gross negligence. This made the *mens rea* of gross negligence much wider than Cunningham subjective recklessness. The *mens rea* of gross negligence manslaughter has been criticised in the cases of *Attorney General's Reference (No. 2 of 1999)* (2000) and *R* v *Misra and Srivastava* (2004).

■ *TIP* Gross negligence manslaughter differs from *constructive manslaughter* in that it can be committed by *omission*. It does not have to be an unlawful act and there must be a risk of death rather than a risk of some harm.

habeas corpus: a Latin term meaning the legal right for a person in *detention* to be brought before a *judge* so that the legality of the detention may be examined

- The detainee must apply to the *High Court* for a writ that orders the detainer to put him or her before a court.
- This allows the detainee to challenge the detention and, if it is unlawful, he or she will be released.

Hansard: a record of the debates in the Houses of *Parliament*.

- Since *Pepper* v *Hart* (1993), *judges* have been allowed to read *Hansard* to try to find the intentions of Parliament when it was debating the law during the *legislation* process. This may aid *statutory interpretation*.
- **TIP** This is an example of an *extrinsic aid*.

harassment: section 1 of the Protection from Harassment Act 1997 (as amended by the Serious Organised Crime and Police Act 2005) states that:

> A person must not pursue a course of conduct…which amounts to harassment
> of another, and…which he knows or ought to know amounts to harassment
> of the other.

- Harassment itself is not defined but includes alarming the person or causing him or her distress. The Act states that 'conduct' includes speech.
- Section 2 of the Protection from Harassment Act 1997 states that the person whose course of conduct is in question ought to know that it amounts to or involves harassment of another if a reasonable person in possession of the same information would think that it amounted to harassment. Thus, a *defendant* would not be able to argue that he or she did not intend to cause the victim harassment if a reasonable person, on the same facts, would realise that it would be the probable result.
- The *statutes* prohibit a 'course of conduct'. When an individual is being harassed, this must involve conduct on at least two occasions. If two or more people are being harassed, a course of conduct means conduct directed at each person on at least one occasion. A person who pursues such a course of conduct is guilty of a criminal offence, but the *legislation* also provides a civil *remedy*.

h

Hart–Devlin debate: opposing viewpoints regarding law and morality that came about following the recommendations of the Wolfenden Report.

■ The Wolfenden Committee was set up in the 1950s to consider the law regarding prostitution and homosexuality. The recommendations were to legalise both. Lord Devlin was strongly opposed to these recommendations, whereas Professor Hart approved of them.

■ Lord Devlin argued that society needs a common morality with basic agreement of what is good and evil, and it is up to the law to uphold this morality. Professor Hart (who was influenced by the writings of *John Stuart Mill*) argued that laws enforcing morals should not be passed because morality would be unable to change and develop over time. He thought that the law should not punish behaviour that simply disgusts others and does not harm anyone.

■ *TIP* Homosexual acts between consenting male adults were not legalised until 1967.

Haseldine v Daw (1941) (*occupiers' liability*)**:** the *claimant* was injured during a visit to a client who lived in the *defendant's* block of flats. His injuries were sustained when the lift malfunctioned and fell to the bottom of the shaft. The malfunction was caused by work that had been carried out by *independent contractors*. The defendant was not held to be liable for the claimant's injuries, as he knew little about the workings of hydraulic lifts, so it was entirely reasonable for him to employ an expert in that area. Additionally, he had used a respected company, with which he had had dealings over many years. The *occupier* had clearly discharged his duty to the *visitor* in this case and therefore was not liable for the injuries.

Hedley Byrne and Co. Ltd v Heller and Partners (1964) (*negligence — pure economic loss*)**:** Hedley Byrne was an advertising agency that was asked to buy advertising space for Easipower Ltd. Before it did, it asked its bank (N&P) to check that Easipower was creditworthy. N&P asked Heller (Easipower's bank) who said that Easipower was 'trustworthy' up to £100,000 per year. Hedley Byrne bought the advertising space for Easipower, but before Easipower paid, it went into liquidation. Hedley Byrne lost £17,000 and sued Heller for giving bad advice. However, Heller was not liable because it had specifically said that its statements were made 'without responsibility', but the *House of Lords* used the opportunity to create a test known as the 'Hedley Byrne principle'. This test decides the circumstances in which a *duty of care* is owed for *negligent misstatement*:

(1) There was a *special relationship* between the *defendant* and the *claimant*.

(2) The claimant relied on the defendant's advice.

(3) It was reasonable to rely on the advice (*Chaudry v Prabhakar,* 1988).

■ The *White* v *Jones* (1995) decision is an exception to the normal rules regarding pure economic loss. This case is said to extend the Hedley Byrne principle. The claimant successfully sued a solicitor whose negligent act prevented the claimant from benefiting from a will.

Heydon's Case (1584): established the *mischief rule* of *statutory interpretation*.

■ When using this rule, a *judge* should consider what the *common law* was before the *Act of Parliament* was passed, what the problem was with that law and what remedy *Parliament* was trying to provide.

hierarchy of the courts (*judicial precedent*)**:** the order of authority in which the courts are placed.

■ Decisions of the superior courts (*House of Lords, Court of Appeal* and *High Court*) have to be followed by the inferior courts (*Crown Court, County Court* and *Magistrates' Court*).

High Court: the court of first instance for trials involving specific areas of law or claims over £15,000 (£50,000 for personal injury claims).

■ It has three divisions that each deal with certain types of civil claims:
  • the *Queen's Bench Division*
  • the *Family Division*
  • the *Chancery Division*

High Court judge: decides cases in the *High Court* and serious cases in the *Crown Court*.

■ High Court judges are known as Mr or Mrs Justice (Surname).

■ Applicants must have had a *right of audience* in relation to all proceedings in the High Court for 10 years or have been a *circuit judge* for at least 2 years. Once appointed, they are assigned to a division of the High Court: the *Chancery Division*, the *Queen's Bench Division* or the *Family Division*.

Hill v Chief Constable of West Yorkshire Police (1988) (*negligence*)**:** the police did not owe a *duty of care* to the mother of a young woman who was murdered by the serial killer Peter Sutcliffe (the 'Yorkshire Ripper').

■ Mrs Hill believed that the police were responsible for her daughter's death because they had failed to catch Sutcliffe quickly enough. The *House of Lords* held that it was not in the public interest for the police to be held accountable to the families of victims for failing to prevent a crime.

■ **TIP** This immunity that the police enjoyed was questioned in the *European Court of Human Rights*, e.g. *Osman* v *UK* (2000) and *Z* v *UK* (2001). As a result of these cases, the courts will not apply blanket immunity to all police officers who are sued for negligence. Since *Brooks* v *Commissioner of the Police for the Metropolis* (2005), each new case is decided on its facts. Failure to prevent a crime does not establish a duty of care, unless the police have 'assumed a responsibility' towards that person (as in *Home Office* v *Dorset Yacht Co. Ltd*, 1970).

homicide: the unlawful killing of a human being.

■ *Murder, voluntary manslaughter* and *involuntary manslaughter* fall into the category of 'homicide'.

h

■ The *Law Commission* report: *Murder, Manslaughter and Infanticide (28 November 2006)* suggested a programme of reform for the current law of homicide. It recommended that the offence of homicide should be changed to *first-degree murder, second-degree murder* and *manslaughter*.

Homicide Act 1957: defines the three partial defences that reduce a charge of *murder* to *voluntary manslaughter*.

■ Section 2 (*diminished responsibility*) states:
> Where a person kills or is party to a killing of another, he shall not be convicted of murder if he was suffering from such abnormality of mind (whether arising from a condition of arrested or retarded development of mind or any inherent causes or induced by disease or injury) as substantially impaired his mental responsibility for his acts and omissions in doing or being a party to the killing.

■ Section 3 (*provocation*) states:
> Where on a charge of murder there is evidence on which the jury can find that the person charged was provoked (whether by things done or by things said or by both together) to lose his self-control, the question whether the provocation was enough to make a reasonable man do as he did shall be left to be determined by the jury; and in determining that question the jury shall take into account everything both done and said according to the effect which, in their opinion, it would have on a reasonable man.

■ Section 4 (*suicide pact*) states:
> It shall be manslaughter and shall not be murder for a person acting in pursuance of a suicide pact between himself and another to kill the other or be a party to the other killing himself or being killed by a third party.

horizontal direct effect: see *direct effect*.

House of Commons: the elected chamber in *Parliament*.

■ It consists of Members of Parliament (MPs) who are members of the *government* and the opposition parties. There is also a speaker who controls the proceedings.

House of Lords (court): the final court of appeal in the UK in both criminal and civil cases.

■ The House of Lords only hears appeals with leave (permission granted by the *Court of Appeal* or the House of Lords) on a point of law of general public importance. It hears both criminal and civil appeals. It also hears appeals from Commonwealth countries in its capacity as the *Judicial Committee of the Privy Council*.

■ Cases concerning human rights issues may be appealed further to the *European Court of Human Rights*. The House of Lords may refer a case concerning *European Union* law to the European Court of Justice for a decision. This is known as an *Article 234 referral*.

House of Lords judge: see *Law Lord*.

h

House of Lords (Parliament): the second chamber in the Houses of Parliament.

■ The House of Lords is made up of unelected peers. Since the House of Lords Act 1999, there are a few remaining hereditary peers with the rest of the House comprising life peers, bishops and the *Law Lords*.

■ Its role in the *legislation* process is to scrutinise a *bill* further. It may suggest amendments, which must be approved by the *House of Commons*. The House of Lords has the power to delay a bill for 1 year (1 month for finance bills) but it cannot prevent a bill being passed. The House of Commons may invoke the *Parliament Act* if it wishes to avoid this delay and bypass the House of Lords.

Human Rights Act 1998: statute incorporating the *European Convention on Human Rights* into UK law to protect the rights of people.

■ The different rights and freedoms conferred by the Act include the right to life, prohibition of torture, prohibition of slavery and forced labour, and the right to liberty and security.

■ Section 19 of the Human Rights Act requires that all new *Acts of Parliament* must state that they are compatible with human rights, and that if a new Act is not compatible, *Parliament* is required to state that this was its intention.

■ Section 3 of the Human Rights Act requires *judges* to interpret the law in light of this Act. If the judge believes that an Act is not compatible with human rights, he or she can make a declaration of incompatibility, suggesting that Parliament make an amendment. However, a judge cannot refuse to follow an Act of Parliament even if it contravenes the Human Rights Act.

■ *TIP* New Acts of Parliament should be compatible with the Human Rights Act, but will still be applied by the courts even if they are not. Parliament can pass laws that are not compatible with the Act if it has taken the Act into account when passing the law.

***Hunter* v *Canary Wharf Ltd and London Docklands Development Corporation* (1995)** (*private nuisance*)**:** an important case that considered whether people without an interest in *land* could make a claim in *nuisance*.

■ Many people were adversely affected by the noise and dust created when the *defendants* built a tower block. By following the decision in *Khoransandjian* v *Bush* (1994), the *Court of Appeal* allowed claims to be made by people who did not have an interest in the land but who were affected by the building of Canary Wharf. However, the *House of Lords* reversed the decision and held that claims could be made only by people who owned or occupied land near to Canary Wharf. This was done in order to simplify the law of nuisance and reaffirm that it is essentially a land-based *tort*.

***ICI* v *Shatwell* (1965)** (*volenti non fit injuria*): two brothers were employed as shot firers in the *defendant's* quarry. In breach of their employer's instructions — and also of *statutes* and safety regulations — they did not follow the correct procedures when testing explosives and were both injured as a result when there was an explosion. The *House of Lords* held that the defence of *volenti non fit injuria* applied here and, as such, the employers were not negligent. The *employees* had undertaken the unsafe method of working entirely of their own accord and in breach of explicit instructions issued by their employer.

idea stage: the first stage of the *legislation* process.

■ The idea for a new law can come from many different sources such as the *Law Commission*, *Royal Commission* reports, *manifesto promises* etc. (see *Law Reform*).

ILEX: see *Institute of Legal Executives*.

implied consent (*volenti non fit injuria*): circumstances or conduct that imply that a person has consented to a risk (see *Smith* v *Baker, 1891* and *ICI* v *Shatwell, 1965*).

■ *e.g.* If a boxer turns up for a fight, his opponent would infer that he has consented to the fight by his conduct — i.e. the fact that he has turned up.

■ Under s.149 of the Road Traffic Act 1988, getting in a person's car does not imply *consent* to injury. However, in *Morris* v *Murray* (1991), getting on an aeroplane with a pilot who was known to have been drinking alcohol was held to imply consent to injury.

■ The courts give special consideration to rescuers and it is rare that the defence of *volenti non fit injuria* will apply. In *Salmon* v *Seafarers' Restaurants* (1983), the fact that the *claimant* was a professional rescuer (a fireman) did not mean that he voluntarily accepted the risk of harm.

implied malice (*murder*): *intention* to cause *grievous bodily harm*.

implied permission (*occupiers' liability*): sometimes a person may not have *express permission* to be on *land* or *premises* but may still be classed as a *visitor* if the courts decide that he or she had implied permission to be there.

- **e.g.** The police, fire brigade, those who need to gain access to read gas, electricity and water meters, and sales people are all taken to have implied permission and are classed as visitors. Those who enter shops are taken to have permission to be there.
- The courts may also infer permission in certain circumstances, e.g. *Lowery v Walker (1911)*.

implied terms: the parts of a *contract* that do not need to be expressly agreed.

- Some terms are implied by the *common law* and by *statute*.
- **e.g.** Section 14(2) of the Sale of Goods Act 1979 states that goods bought from a business must be of a 'satisfactory quality'.

inchoate offences: preliminary offences such as *attempts, conspiracy* and *incitement*.

- Although these do not constitute complete offences, they are still prohibited by the criminal law because they constitute steps towards the complete offence.

incitement (*inchoate offences*)**:** encouraging someone to commit a crime.

- This can include suggestion, persuasion and even threats (*Race Relations Board v Applin*, 1973). It can be committed by actions or words.
- Incitement can still be committed even when the offence is impossible to commit (*R* v *Fitzmaurice*, 1983).
- Incitement of an *indictable offence* such as *murder* is punishable with life imprisonment. Incitement of a *summary offence* carries the same sentence as the summary offence.
- **TIP** Incitement is an inchoate offence, which means that the full offence was not committed.

independent contractor (*occupiers' liability*)**:** section 2(4)(b) of the *Occupiers' Liability Act 1957* states that:

> Where damage is caused to a visitor by a danger due to the faulty execution of any work of construction, maintenance or repair by an independent contractor employed by the occupier, the occupier is not to be treated...as answerable for the danger if in all the circumstances he had acted reasonably in entrusting the work to an independent contractor and had taken such steps (if any) as he reasonably ought in order to satisfy himself that the contractor was competent and that the work had been properly done.

- An *occupier* will not be liable for the faulty work of an independent contractor, as long as it was reasonable to hire an independent contractor and the occupier had taken reasonable care to check both that the contractor was competent and that the work was done properly.
- **e.g.** See *Haseldine* v *Daw (1941)*.

independent contractor (*vicarious liability*)**:** a person who employs an independent contractor will not usually be responsible for any *torts* committed by the contractor.

■ There are, however, circumstances where an employer will be responsible, e.g. if the independent contractor is carrying out work that is inherently dangerous, such as working on the motorway.

indictable offence: crimes that must be tried at the *Crown Court*.

■ These are the most serious offences, e.g. murder.

indirect intention: see *oblique intention*.

individualised sentence: a punishment that is selected according to the offender's specific circumstances.

■ The *judge* may believe that the *tariff system* of sentencing is not appropriate in a particular case and instead choose a sentence that most suits the individual.

■ Repeat offenders (known as recidivists) may receive an individualised sentence if the tariff sentence has not acted as a *deterrent*.

■ *e.g.* If a shoplifter is fined according to the tariff guidelines each time he or she is caught, an individualised sentence such as a suspended *custodial sentence* may work better as a deterrent.

induced by disease or injury (*diminished responsibility*)**:** an *abnormality of mind* that is caused by physical or mental disease, or injuries such as brain damage resulting from being hit on the head.

■ Alcohol or drugs will not usually give rise to an abnormality of mind unless they have caused brain damage (see *R v Tandy, 1989*).

influences on Parliament: see *law reform*.

inherent cause (*diminished responsibility*)**:** an internal cause of the *defendant's abnormality of mind*.

■ *e.g.* Epilepsy, premenstrual tension, *battered women's syndrome* and shock are inherent causes. Depression due to a chemical imbalance in the brain is accepted as an inherent cause, but not if it is caused by a reaction to an event, as this would be an external cause (see *R v Dietschmann, 2003*).

injunction: a court order that either forces the *defendant* to stop a certain activity (prohibitory injunction) or makes him or her carry out a certain act (mandatory injunction).

■ An injunction can also be full (a total ban on the *tort*) or partial (the tort can be permitted in certain circumstances).

■ The court will not grant an injunction if *damages* would be more appropriate. The court may also award damages as well as an injunction.

■ *TIP* In the *tort* of *nuisance*, injunctions are a common *remedy*.

Inns of Court: four legal societies, one of which a *barrister* must join.

■ The four Inns of Court are Gray's Inn, Lincoln's Inn, Inner Temple and Middle Temple, which are all based in London. Students taking the *Bar Vocational Course* must dine at their Inn 12 times before being called to the Bar.

■ The Inns also provide scholarships, law libraries and accommodation for barristers' *chambers* and can discipline barristers if a complaint is made against them.

insane automatism: a defence based on the *defendant* having a *disease of the mind,* which is treated in the same way as *insanity.*

■ It includes situations where the defendant commits a crime while having a reflex action or a fit that is due to an internal cause (see *Bratty* v *Attorney General for Northern Ireland, 1963*).

insanity (also known as *insane automatism*)**:** a defence based on the *defendant's defect of reason.*

■ To be held criminally liable, a defendant must be deemed sane. The current rules regarding insanity came from the case of *R* v *M'Naghten (1843).*

■ In order to establish a defence on the grounds of insanity, it must be clearly proved that at the time of committing the act the defendant was labouring under such a defect of reason, caused by a *disease of the mind,* that he or she did not know the nature and quality of the act or did not know that what he or she was doing was legally wrong.

■ If a plea of insanity is successful, it leads to a special verdict and the defendant will be deemed 'not guilty by reason of insanity'.

■ The defence of insanity for a charge of *murder* results in an indefinite hospital stay. Under the *Criminal Procedure Act 1991,* for crimes other than murder the judge can make a hospital order, a guardianship order, a supervision and treatment order or an absolute discharge.

Institute of Legal Executives (ILEX): the governing body of *legal executives.*

■ ILEX is also the name given to the examinations taken by a legal executive.

intangible property (*theft*)**:** *property* that does not physically exist but gives the owner legal rights.

■ It includes money in a bank account, debts, shares and intellectual property such as copyright.

■ See *Oxford* v *Moss (1979).*

integration test (*vicarious liability*)**:** if a person's work is an integral part of the employer's business, this may prove that he or she is an *employee* (*Stevenson, Jordan and Harrison Ltd* v *Macdonald and Evans,* 1952).

■ *e.g.* A person employed to work on the till in a shop would usually be an employee. However, if the till was broken, the person called in to fix it would probably be an *independent contractor,* as his or her work would be incidental to the business of running the shop.

intention (*mens rea*)**:** the *defendant's* aim or plan to bring about a particular consequence.

■ Establishing the defendant's intention uses a *subjective test* to decide what he or she was thinking while committing the *actus reus* of a crime. The defendant may have *direct intention* or *oblique intention* (also known as indirect intention).

■ Crimes that can only be committed with the *mens rea* of intention are known as *specific intent* crimes.

■ *e.g.* The *mens rea* of *murder* is intention to kill or cause really serious harm.

intention to create legal relations: the requirement that changes an agreement into a legally enforceable *contract*.

■ There is a presumption that agreements between family and friends are not legally enforceable contracts. In *Merritt* v *Merritt* (1970), there was a contract between a separated husband and wife, who agreed that the husband would sign over the house to his wife when she had paid off the mortgage. However, in *Balfour* v *Balfour* (1919) there was no contract formed when a husband promised to send his wife money while he was away and did not.

■ The courts decide that there is an intention to create legal relations in most business agreements.

intention to permanently deprive (*theft*)**:** part of the *mens rea* of theft, defined in s.6(1) of the *Theft Act 1968* as:

> A person appropriating property belonging to another without meaning the other permanently to lose the thing itself is nevertheless to be regarded as having the intention of permanently depriving the other of it if his intention is to treat the thing as his own to dispose of regardless of the other's rights; and a borrowing or lending of it may amount to so treating it if, but only if, the borrowing or lending is for a period and in circumstances making it equivalent to an outright taking or disposal.

■ In *R* v *Velumyl* (1989), a company director took money from the safe with the intention of paying it back. He was found guilty of theft because he would not return the exact money that he took. Instead, he would replace it with different money of the same value. He was not entitled to take the money and it did not matter that he was going to pay it back.

■ In *R* v *Lloyd and Others* (1985), the *defendant* worked at a cinema. He gave the films to his friends to copy and then returned them straightaway. There was no theft because the films had not reduced in value, they were not in a changed state, and the defendant did not intend to permanently deprive the owner of them.

interference (*private nuisance*)**:** e.g. smoke, noise, smell, roots etc.

■ The interference must be indirect (e.g. noise on one piece of *land* that affects the people living next door) as opposed to direct interference (where the *defendant* has come onto the *claimant's* land).

■ It was not classed as interference when a newly erected tower-block building disrupted the television reception of residents living nearby (*Hunter* v *Canary Wharf,* 1997).

interference (*trespass to land*)**:** must be direct (*Esso Petroleum Co.* v *Southport Corporation,* 1956).

■ The interference must continue all the time that it is on the *land* (*Holmes* v *Wilson,* 1839).

■ Objects that overhang the land may amount to be trespass (*Woolerton and Wilson* v *Richard Costain Ltd,* 1970 and *Kelsen* v *Imperial Tobacco Co. Ltd,* 1956).

- A lawful *visitor* may become a *trespasser* by going beyond his or her permission to be on land or by staying on the land longer than he or she should. If the *defendant* has a lawful right to be on the land (granted by *common law* or *statute*) but then becomes a trespasser by committing a wrongful act, this is known as trespass *ab initio* (*Six Carpenters*, 1610).
- Throwing something onto the land or allowing animals onto the land will amount to trespass (*League Against Cruel Sports Ltd* v *Scott*, 1986).

Interpretation Act 1978: an aid to *statutory interpretation*, which states that masculine identities include feminine identities, and singular includes plural.

- *e.g.* If an *Act of Parliament* states that it applies to dangerous dogs, it also applies to a single dog and female dogs.

intoxication: to prove this defence, the *defendant* must show that alcohol, drugs, or a combination of the two made him or her incapable of forming the *mens rea* of the relevant offence.

- The effect of the intoxication must be to render the defendant incapable of anticipating any of the consequences of his or her actions. Therefore, the defence applies only in limited circumstances, where the effect of the intoxication was extreme. If, despite his or her intoxicated state, the defendant was still able to form *mens rea*, then the defence will not apply (see *R* v *Kingston, 1994*).
- The leading case of *DPP* v *Majewski (1977)* made a distinction between *specific intent* crimes and *basic intent* crimes. The courts also draw a distinction between *voluntary intoxication* and *involuntary intoxication*.
- If the defendant is voluntarily intoxicated and incapable of forming *mens rea*, he or she will have a defence to specific intent crimes but not basic intent crimes. If the defendant is charged with a specific intent crime that does not have a corresponding basic intent crime (e.g. *theft*), intoxication can provide a complete defence. If the defendant is involuntarily intoxicated and incapable of forming *mens rea*, he or she will have a defence to both basic intent and specific intent crimes.
- The burden of proof rests with the defendant, who must provide some evidence of intoxication before the defence can be put before the *jury*. It is then up to the prosecution to prove *beyond reasonable doubt* that, despite this evidence, the defendant still formed the necessary *mens rea*.

intrinsic aids (also known as 'internal aids'): sources within an *Act of Parliament* that may aid a *judge* in trying to interpret the law.

- To determine the meaning of a section of an Act of Parliament, the judge may wish to look at other sections in the Act: the definition section, preamble and the long and short title.

invitation to treat: an invitation to others to make offers.

- The display of goods in a shop is not an offer, but is instead merely an invitation for the customer to make an offer that the shopkeeper will decide to accept or decline.

- **e.g.** In *Fisher* v *Bell (1961)*, the display of a flick-knife was seen as an invitation to treat. Goods displayed on the shelves of a supermarket are also an invitation to treat according to *Pharmaceutical SGB* v *Boots Cash Chemists* (1953).

involuntary intoxication: where a *defendant* does not know that he or she is taking alcohol or an intoxicating drug.

- If the defendant is involuntarily intoxicated, he or she will have a defence to both *specific intent* and *basic intent* crimes, as long as he or she did not form the required *mens rea*.
- **e.g.** The defendant unknowingly had his or her drink 'spiked', and so was unaware that he or she was consuming drugs or alcohol; the defendant took prescription drugs; or the defendant had an unexpected reaction to soporific drugs (see *R* v *Hardie, 1984*).

involuntary manslaughter: a criminal offence with the same *actus reus* as *murder* (*unlawful killing*) but with a different *mens rea*.

- Murder requires an *intention* to kill or to cause *grievous bodily harm*, whereas involuntary manslaughter does not state what the required *mens rea* is, apart from that it is something other than an intention to kill or to cause grievous bodily harm.
- There are two types of involuntary manslaughter: *constructive manslaughter* and *gross negligence manslaughter*. Subjective *reckless manslaughter* was applied in the case of *R* v *Lidar (1999)*, as it was not a separate type of involuntary manslaughter, just an aspect of gross negligence manslaughter.
- **TIP** Involuntary manslaughter is a *common-law* offence.

John Stuart Mill: exponent of the theory of *utilitarianism*. (Also see *Hart–Devlin debate*.)

■ He believed that the *government* should not impose rules on individuals. Instead, individuals should be free to do what they want, as long as their actions do not harm anyone else. Mill described drug taking and prostitution as 'victimless' crimes, which should, therefore, be legalised.

■ His views on abortion and homosexuality met with much criticism.

Joint Charging Standards: guidelines produced by the police and *Crown Prosecution Service* to define the type of injuries necessary to constitute *common assault, actual bodily harm* and *grievous bodily harm*.

■ Common assault: minor bruising, grazing, small cuts and swelling.

■ Actual bodily harm: minor fractures (such as a broken nose), severe bruising, loss of consciousness, small cuts that require stitches and psychiatric injury.

■ Grievous bodily harm: serious injuries, broken bones, dislocated joints and injury causing permanent disability or disfigurement.

***Jolley* v *Sutton LBC* (2000)** (*occupiers' liability*): a 14-year-old boy was paralysed when an abandoned boat fell onto him. The council knew the boat had been abandoned near a block of flats but failed to remove it, and the *House of Lords* decided that it was liable for the *claimant's* injuries even though they were more severe than expected.

judge: a legal professional who administers justice in the courts.

■ In criminal cases, judges must ensure that the *jury* understands the law that it is being asked to apply. The judge must also pass an appropriate sentence when required.

■ In civil law, where the use of juries is much reduced, cases are often heard by a judge alone, and it is the judge who decides on both the law and the facts. Whatever the type of case, judges must ensure that they remain independent and impartial at all times.

■ Judges also play a role in making law, which is done through *judicial precedent* and *statutory interpretation*.

■ Judges are recruited from *solicitors* and *barristers*.

Judicial Appointments Commission: responsible for the selection and recruitment of *judges*.

◼ Set up by the Constitutional Reform Act 2005, it is an independent body that selects candidates for judicial office. It took over this role from the *Lord Chancellor* in April 2006.

◼ It is made up of 15 commissioners, some of whom have a legal background — as members of the *judiciary, lawyers* or *tribunals* — while others, including the chairperson, are members of the public.

◼ *TIP* The introduction of the Judicial Appointments Commission was designed to make the judicial appointments system more transparent, as it has been criticised in the past for being shrouded in secrecy.

Judicial Committee of the Privy Council: the court that decides cases involving Commonwealth countries.

◼ The *judges* of the *House of Lords* sometimes sit as a final appeal court for cases in countries such as Australia. The decisions made by the Judicial Committee of the Privy Council have, in the past, been considered *persuasive precedent*. However, the *Privy Council* decision in *Attorney General for Jersey* v *Holley (2005)* was considered to be a *binding precedent* by the *Court of Appeal* in *R* v *James* (2006).

judicial independence: the ability of *judges* to make decisions without pressure from the *government*.

◼ In 2007, the government is planning the introduction of a supreme court, so that the *Law Lords* will no longer sit in the Houses of *Parliament*. This will allow the Law Lords to be more independent.

judicial inquiry: see *public inquiry*.

judicial precedent: the system whereby *judges* follow their previous decisions.

◼ The system of precedent ensures that there is a consistent application of *common law* in the courts. There are two types of precedent: *binding precedent* and *persuasive precedent*.

◼ Judicial precedent relies on the *hierarchy of the courts*, where judges follow the previous decisions of 'higher' courts to enforce the law.

judicial review: a challenge made to a piece of *delegated legislation* in the *High Court*.

◼ The *judge* will interpret the wording of the *enabling Act* to decide if the law was made *ultra vires* (beyond the powers granted by *Parliament*) and, if it was, it will be declared void.

◼ Under the *Civil Procedure Rules 1999*, an application for judicial review must be made within 3 months. The person or organisation making the application must also have a legal interest (*locus standi*) in the outcome of the case. This legal interest was extended to include pressure groups in *R* v *Her Majesty's Inspectorate of Pollution ex parte Greenpeace* (1994).

Judicial Studies Board: the board responsible for the training of *judges* and *magistrates*.

J

- **e.g.** Judges must attend an induction course and observe trials and case management in court. Criminal judges will visit *prisons* and *young offenders' institutions*. Training continues for all judges throughout their career, and judges in the *Crown Court, County Court* and *High Court* must attend a residential course once every 3 years to keep them informed of changes in both law and procedure.

judiciary: the collective term for *judges*.

jurisdiction: the power of the court.

- **e.g.** The *Magistrates' Court* has the power to sentence up to 12 months' imprisonment (for two offences) or a £5,000 fine.

jurisprudence: the theoretical and philosophical study of law.

jury: a group of 12 members of the public who are selected to decide the outcome in certain criminal and civil cases.

- Juries are mostly used to decide criminal cases at the *Crown Court*, where they determine whether the *defendant* is guilty or not guilty according to the facts of the case. Juries may be used in civil cases such as *defamation*, where they will decide which person is liable.

- Jurors are selected at random from the electoral role and must be aged between 18 and 70 years old.

- **TIP** Certain people are ineligible for jury service, e.g. those who are mentally ill and those with certain criminal convictions.

jus tertii: see *trespass to land*.

justices of the peace: another name for a *magistrate*.

- Magistrates have the initials JP after their name.

keeper (*liability for animals*)**:** the 'keeper' of an animal is responsible for its actions.

■ The keeper is defined in s.2(1) of the *Animals Act 1971* as the person who:

(a) owns the animal or has it in his possession; or

(b) is the head of a household of which a member under the age of sixteen owns the animal or has it in his possession.

■ Under s.2(1):

Where any damage is caused by an animal which belongs to a dangerous species, any person who is a keeper of the animal is liable for the damage, except as otherwise provided by this Act.

King's Counsel: the term that replaces *Queen's Counsel* when there is a male monarch.

King's peace (*Coke's definition of murder*)**:** killing another person would not amount to *murder* if that person is an enemy during wartime.

■ Today, it is under the *Queen's peace*.

■ If the *defendant* is a British citizen, he or she can be tried in the UK for murder committed in another country.

land (*trespass to land*)**:** includes the soil, things attached to the soil such as buildings and crops, the ground beneath the soil, the boundary and even the airspace above the soil that is necessary for the enjoyment of land (e.g. *Bernstein* v *Skyviews*, 1978).

■ Cranes and advertising boards count as trespass to land (*Woolerton and Wilson* v *Richard Costain Ltd*, 1970 and *Kelsen* v *Imperial Tobacco Co. Ltd*, 1956).

■ Under-soil rights may extend under a highway (e.g. *Harrison* v *Duke of Rutland*, 1893 and *Hickman* v *Maisey*, 1900).

Law Commission: an organisation that identifies areas of law where reform is necessary, codifies the law, repeals obsolete laws, and consolidates and modernises the law.

■ The Law Commission Act 1965 set up this permanent body. It consists of five legal experts chosen from the *judiciary*, legal profession and legal academics. It is asked to consider specific areas of law referred to it by the *Lord Chancellor* and may also choose other areas itself to consider. The Law Commission first researches the law it is considering and then produces a consultation paper to allow experts and politicians to comment. It then produces a final report, which includes a draft *bill* if it considers a change to the current law is necessary.

■ Some Law Commission reports have been successful and include the Computer Misuse Act 1990 and the Family Law Act 1996.

■ *Parliament* is not always keen to find time to pass the Law Commission's draft bills.

lawful justification (*trespass to land*)**:** when a person has a right to enter the *claimant's land*.

■ This right may be conferred by *statute,* e.g. the *Police and Criminal Evidence Act 1984* allows the police entry onto land, and the Rights of Entry (Gas and Electricity Boards) Act 1954 allows meter readings to be taken. There may be a *common law* right to enter the land (e.g. to abate a *nuisance*), or a right to go on land that is conferred by prescription (where someone gains a right to do something because of long use).

Law Lord: one of the twelve *judges* who decide cases in the *House of Lords* and *Judicial Committee of the Privy Council*.

■ Law Lords are also known as Lords of Appeal in Ordinary.

■ They are appointed by the queen, on the recommendation of the prime minister, who has been advised by the *Lord Chancellor*.

■ They are appointed from those who hold high judicial office, e.g. a judge in the *Court of Appeal*, or from those with 15 years' experience of Supreme Courts.

law reform: the process of changing the law.

■ The *government* may be influenced by organisations to change existing laws or to make new ones. It may seek the advice of different organisations to help it formulate its policy.

■ There are official law reform agencies such as the *Law Commission* and *Royal Commission*, which suggest proposals for law reform to the government.

■ Other factors for consideration include *media influence, public inquiries, pressure groups* and *manifesto promises*.

Law Reform (Year and a Day Rule) Act 1996: statute that abolished the *year and a day* rule.

■ If the victim of a crime dies more than 3 years after the crime took place and it can be shown that the *defendant* was still the main cause of the death, permission is needed from the *Attorney General* for the case to go to court.

■ If the defendant has already been prosecuted in relation to the incident — probably for a *non-fatal offence* — the Attorney General's consent is also required for a subsequent charge of *murder*.

■ *TIP* This Act was made as a result of a *private members' bill* put forward by Doug Hoyle.

***Lawrence v Metropolitan Police Commissioner* (1972)** (*theft*)**:** an *appropriation* can take place even with the *consent* of the victim.

■ An Italian student who spoke little English got into a taxi in London. The student showed the *defendant* (the taxi driver) an address written down. At the end of the journey the fare was 52p, and the victim offered the taxi driver £1. The driver stated it was not enough, so the victim opened his wallet and the defendant took out another £6 with the victim's permission. The *House of Lords* unanimously decided that this amounted to theft, despite the victim's consent.

law report: the written judgement of a case.

■ Law reports are important because they allow *judges* to find previous decisions and *precedents* of cases that have gone before.

■ The internet allows judges, *lawyers* and legal students to find law reports quickly. They are also printed and stored in law libraries.

Law Society: the governing body for *solicitors*.

■ The Law Society was set up in 1842 to represent the interests of solicitors. Its role includes overseeing training and qualifications, and ensuring that solicitors carrying out publicly funded work are receiving adequate payment. Since 2006, regulatory matters have become the responsibility of the Regulation Board, which is made up of *lay people* and solicitors.

■ The Law Society may investigate complaints made against solicitors. It has the power to reduce the solicitor's bill, order the solicitor to pay compensation of up to £15,000 or tell him or her to correct the mistake and meet any costs incurred. The Office of the Legal Services Complaints Commissioner was set up following the Access To Justice Act 1999. It works with the Law Society and represents the interests of consumers to improve complaints handling.

lawyer: a term used to describe a legal professional, e.g. *solicitors* and *barristers*.

lay people: people who are involved in the legal system but who do not have formal legal qualifications.

■ *e.g.* *Magistrates* and *jury* members are lay people.

■ 'Trial by peers' was considered to be a fair way to administer justice and was mentioned in the *Magna Carta* in 1215.

leapfrog appeal: an appeal made from the *High Court* directly to the *House of Lords* (missing the *Court of Appeal*).

■ Such an appeal may be allowed if the *Court of Appeal* is already bound by one of its previous decisions (see *judicial precedent*).

legal aid: payment of legal costs from public funds for those unable to meet the costs themselves (see *Legal Services Commission*).

■ *e.g.* Criminal legal aid covers those suspected or accused of a criminal offence and enables them to access such advice and representation as required.

legal adviser: a *solicitor* or *barrister* who advises *magistrates* about the law.

■ Legal advisers were previously known as court clerks.

■ Magistrates are *lay people* and therefore require a legally qualified person to help them make decisions.

■ *TIP* It is sometimes argued that magistrates are too reliant on their legal advisers.

legal causation: the *defendant's* conduct must have made a 'significant contribution' to the resulting crime.

■ The defendant's actions do not need to be the only or even the main cause of the harm (known as the *de minimis* rule, whereby the defendant's actions were a more than minimal cause of the result).

■ The chain of causation is where there may be more than one factor contributing to the final result. For the defendant to be guilty, there must be an unbroken chain of causation directly from his or her actions to the end result.

■ The chain of causation may be affected by a number of factors: the actions of the victim (see *R v Roberts 1978*), the actions of a third party (see *R v Pagett, 1983*), or palpably wrong medical treatment (see *R v Jordan, 1956*). One thing that will never break the chain of causation is the susceptibility of the victim (see *R v Blaue, 1975*).

legal executive: a legal professional who works in a *solicitor's* office.

■ Legal executives are able to undertake most of the duties of a solicitor. Any work they do will be under the supervision of the solicitor for whom they work.

■ The *Institute of Legal Executives* (ILEX) governs the training of legal executives.

■ A suitably qualified legal executive may be accepted on the *Legal Practice Course* and train to be a solicitor without having first taken a degree.

legal personality: the legal rights of human beings and corporations.

■ Human beings have legal rights from birth to death. These rights may differ, e.g. minors have fewer legal rights than adults. A foetus does not have a separate legal personality from its mother (see *Attorney General's Reference No. 3, 1994*).

■ A corporation has a separate legal personality from the people who run it. For example, a corporation may own *property* and make *contracts* in its own right. It also means that the people who run the corporation will not personally be financially responsible if the corporation gets into financial difficulties.

Legal Practice Course (LPC): the qualification taken after a degree that allows someone to practise as a *solicitor*.

■ This vocational course lasts 1 year full time or 2 years part time. It provides practical skills such as problem solving, accounts, drafting, advising, ethics and legal research.

legal profession: a profession that consists of legally qualified personnel who work in the legal system.

■ *e.g.* *Barristers* and *solicitors*, *legal executives* and *judges* are legal professionals.

■ *Lawyers* in the British legal system are split into two branches: solicitors and barristers. Both have different routes to qualification, differing roles and separate governing bodies. This division stems from the nineteenth century and the twin monopolies that the professions held over the types of work that they could undertake. Under these monopolies, solicitors had exclusive rights to conduct *litigation* and to carry out *conveyancing*, while barristers monopolised *rights of audience* in the higher courts. The *Courts and Legal Services Act 1990* changed the role of solicitors and barristers.

■ Debates have raged over the need for two branches of the legal profession. This is known as the *fusion debate*.

Legal Services Commission (LSC): an organisation in charge of administering *legal aid* in England and Wales.

■ The LSC administers two different schemes, depending on whether it is a civil or a criminal matter. The *Community Legal Service* deals with civil legal aid, while criminal legal aid is administered by the *Criminal Defence Service*.

■ *TIP* The LSC was established under the Access To Justice Act 1999 and replaced the old legal aid scheme.

Legal Services Ombudsman (LSO): investigates complaints about the way in which a professional body in the legal services handled a complaint made to it about one of its members.

■ If a client has complained about a *solicitor* or *barrister* to the relevant governing bodies (the *Law Society* and the *Bar Council* respectively) but was unsuccessful, he or she can make a final appeal to the LSO within 3 months of receiving the Law Society or Bar Council's decision.

■ The powers of the LSO include recommending that the Law Society or Bar Council reconsider the complaint, formally criticising the Law Society or Bar Council, or ordering them to pay compensation.

legislation: the process by which *Parliament* makes laws.

■ Parliament is made up of the *House of Commons*, the *House of Lords* and the monarch, and all three have a role in the legislation process.

■ The *government* controls the legislative agenda (what laws are to be made) but it may get its ideas from influences on Parliament (see *law reform*).

■ The four main stages of the legislation process are the *idea stage*, *consultation stage*, *drafting stage*, and *parliamentary stage*.

■ *TIP* The most important stage in the legislation process is the *parliamentary stage*.

Leonesio v Italian Ministry of Agriculture (1973): an example of an EU *regulation* having a vertical *direct effect*.

■ A regulation stated that *member states* should subsidise dairy farmers who do not produce milk for 5 years (to reduce over-production). Leonesio claimed his money from the Italian *government* but it refused to pay him because it had not passed a law allowing such compensation to be paid. The court held that Leonesio was entitled to his money. The regulation did not require the Italian government to change its laws. The regulation immediately becomes part of the member state's law the moment it is passed by the *European Union*.

liability for animals: this may arise under the *common law* or under the statutory rules contained in the *Animals Act 1971*.

■ The common law rules relating to liability for animals were replaced by the Animals Act 1971. It is possible, however, to bring a successful action in other *torts*: *negligence* (*Draper* v *Hodder*, 1972); *nuisance* (*Pitcher* v *Martin*, 1937; see *Rylands* v *Fletcher, 1868*). Trespass to goods, *trespass to land* and *trespass to the person* may also be successful.

■ *TIP* The law relating to animals is *strict liability*.

liability for injury to livestock caused by dogs: section 9 of the *Animals Act 1971* makes it lawful to kill or injure a dog that:

    (i) is worrying or is about to worry livestock, and there is no other reasonable means of ending or preventing the worrying; or

    (ii) has been worrying livestock, has not left the vicinity, is not under the control of any person and there are no practicable means of ascertaining to whom it belongs.

■ Under s.3 of the Animals Act 1971, the *keeper* of a dog that causes damage by killing or injuring *livestock* will be liable for *damages* unless he or she can prove a defence.

libel: see *defamation*.

***Limpus* v *London General Omnibus Co.* (1862)** (*vicarious liability*): an employer may be vicariously liable if his or her *employee* does an authorised act but in an unauthorised way.

■ Bus drivers were given a card stating that they 'must not on any account race with or obstruct another omnibus'. A driver employed by the *defendants* ignored the instructions on the card and obstructed another bus, causing an accident. The employers were vicariously liable because the *damage* resulted from the driver doing an authorised act (driving the bus) albeit in an unauthorised way.

***Lister* v *Hesley Hall* (2001)** (*vicarious liability*): the *claimants* were pupils at a boarding school for children with emotional and behavioural difficulties. While there, they were sexually abused by the warden. He was imprisoned and the claimants brought claims for personal injury against his employers. The *House of Lords* said that the key question was whether the warden's *torts* were so closely connected with his employment that it would be fair and just to hold the employers vicariously liable. It decided that, on the facts of the case, the *defendants* were vicariously liable since the sexual abuse was 'inextricably interwoven with the carrying out by the warden of his duties'.

literal rule (of *statutory interpretation*): where a *judge* takes the ordinary and natural meaning of a word in an *Act of Parliament* and applies it, even if it creates an absurd result.

■ This rule respects parliamentary *sovereignty*.

■ Lord Esher said in 1892: 'The court has nothing to do with the question of whether the legislature has committed an absurdity.'

■ The leading case for the literal rule is *Fisher v Bell (1961)*. It was also applied in the cases of *Whitely v Chapell* (1868), *London and North Eastern Railway Co. v Berriman* (1946) and, more recently, in *R v Bentham* (2005).

litigation: resolving a legal dispute in court.

livestock: see *trespassing livestock*.

locality (*private nuisance*): the type of area where the *interference* occurs may affect whether it is regarded as *unreasonable*.

■ People who live in the country should expect certain noises and smells, in the same way that someone who lives in the city would, e.g. *Sturges v Bridgman (1879)*.

■ *TIP* The locality will not be significant if the claimant has suffered physical damage (*St Helens Smelting Co. Ltd v Tipping*, 1865).

locus standi: see *judicial review*.

Lord Chancellor: the former head of the *judiciary*.

■ The *Lord Chief Justice* took over this role from the Lord Chancellor on 3 April 2006. The remaining roles of the Lord Chancellor have been taken over by the Secretary of State for Constitutional Affairs.

■ The appointment of the judiciary was the responsibility of the Lord Chancellor, but it has now been taken over by the *Judicial Appointments Commission*.

■ **TIP** The position of Lord Chancellor was changed because it was not compatible with the theory of the *separation of powers*.

Lord Chief Justice: the *judge* who is head of the *judiciary* and President of the Courts.

■ The Lord Chief Justice took over these roles from the *Lord Chancellor* on 3 April 2006. The role carries over 400 duties, but the main ones include the training and guidance of judges, representing the judiciary in *Parliament*, giving judgements in important cases, dealing with complaints made against judges and chairing the *Sentencing Guidelines Council*, which issues guidelines to courts on appropriate *sentencing* practice.

■ The current Lord Chief Justice is Lord Phillips of Worth Matravers. The next Lord Chief Justice will be appointed by the *Judicial Appointments Commission* and will probably be selected from the Appeal Court judges. The candidate could also be selected from among the *Law Lords*.

Lord of Appeal in Ordinary: see *Law Lord*.

Lord Woolf: the *judge* who wrote the *Access to Justice Report 1996*.

loss of self-control (*provocation*): the *provocative conduct* must make the *defendant* have a sudden and temporary loss of self-control.

■ This is the second requirement for proving the partial defence of provocation. The *jury* must decide, using a *subjective test*, that the defendant was provoked to lose his or her self-control as a matter of fact. There should be no *cooling-off period*, as this gives the defendant time to think about his or her actions.

■ According to *R v Duffy* (1949), loss of self-control must be 'sudden and temporary' and is the same as a loss of temper (see *R v Cocker, 1989*).

■ **TIP** This requirement has caused problems for the courts when dealing with those suffering from *battered women's syndrome* (see *R v Thornton (No. 1), 1992* and *R v Ahluwalia, 1992*). The courts have tried to solve this problem with the concept of *cumulative provocation*. In *R v Ahluwalia (1992)*, the *Court of Appeal* stated that a time delay did not automatically mean that the defence would fail, as the defendant might still have had a sudden and temporary loss of self-control at the last moment.

Lowery v Walker (1911) (*occupiers' liability*): for 35 years, people had used the *defendant* farmer's unfenced field as a short cut to the station. The defendant had asked them repeatedly not to do this but had taken no further action for fear that people would stop buying milk from him. He then put a wild horse in the field and the *claimant* was injured when the horse attacked. The courts held that, despite the fact that the farmer had asked people not to use the field as a short cut, the claimant did have *implied permission* to be there and thus was to be classed as a *visitor* rather than a *trespasser*.

LPC: see *Legal Practice Course*.

LSC: see *Legal Services Commission*.

LSO: see *Legal Services Ombudsman*.

***Macarthys v Smith* (1979):** an example of a treaty having a horizontal *direct effect*.

■ Smith challenged her employer under *European Union* law for paying her male predecessor a higher wage for the same job. Her case was successful.

magistrates: *lay people* who decide cases at the *Magistrates' Court*.

■ Magistrates are not legally qualified and are not paid for their work. Their main role is to decide criminal cases involving a *summary offence*, preliminary matters in more serious cases, and cases involving *young offenders*.

■ They are involved in civil cases such as non-payment of council tax. There is also a family court that deals with matters involving children.

■ A magistrate must be aged between 18 and 65 and of good character. Applicants apply to the *Lord Chancellor* and are interviewed by a Local Advisory Committee..

Magistrates' Court: deals mainly with criminal cases, yet it has some civil *jurisdiction* over family matters.

■ All criminal cases start at the Magistrates' Court. It deals with preliminary matters such as *bail* applications and *legal aid*. It has the power to try all *summary offences* and may try *either-way offences* if the *defendant* chooses to have the case heard at the Magistrates' Court. The *magistrates* have the power to sentence a defendant to up to 12 months' imprisonment (for two offences). They can also fine the defendant up to £5,000. If the magistrates accept jurisdiction in an either-way offence and then wish to sentence the defendant to longer than 12 months in prison, they will send the case to the *Crown Court* for sentencing. *Indictable offences* are sent to the Crown Court for trial. The Magistrates' Court also has specially trained magistrates who deal with *young offenders* in the *Youth Court*.

■ In its civil role, the Magistrates' Court can approve care orders and adoption orders for children and make provisions for the break up of a marriage. (However, it cannot grant a divorce.) Magistrates are also involved in licensing and the enforcement of non-payment of council tax.

Magna Carta (also known as 'Magna Carta Libertatum' — 'Great Charter of Freedoms'): an English charter signed by King John in 1215 that set out many rules concerning the powers of the monarch and the Church. It also included rights such as 'trial by peers', which led to the establishment of trials by *jury* and the *Magistrates' Court*.

■ *TIP* The Magna Carta influenced many documents including the US Constitution and Bill of Rights. It is considered one of the most important legal documents in the history of democracy.

Maguire v Harland and Wolff PLC (2005) (*negligence — duty of care*)**:** the *claimant* became ill from exposure to asbestos that her husband had on his work clothes. She tried to claim compensation from his employers. This case dates back to 1965, when the dangers of asbestos were not known. It was not foreseeable that she would get ill and therefore her husband's employers did not owe a duty of care.

making off without payment: defined in s.3 of the *Theft Act 1978* as:

> A person who, knowing that payment on the spot for any goods supplied or services done is required or expected from him, dishonestly makes off without having paid as required or expected and with intent to avoid payment.

■ There are three parts to the *actus reus* for this offence:

(1) Making off: the actual spot that the *defendant* 'makes off' from is usually the place or point where payment is required (*R* v *McDavitt*, 1981).

(2) Without payment: the payment must be required or expected at the time that the defendant makes off. If the defendant makes an agreement that he or she will pay for the goods or services at a later date, the offence has not been committed (*R* v *Vincent*, 2001).

(3) Goods supplied or services done: the goods and services must be ones where payment is legally enforceable. Section 3(3) states that there is no offence when the goods or services are against the law. For example, it would not be an offence to make off without paying a drug dealer. The most commonly used examples of 'goods supplied or services done' are when a person fills up his or her car with petrol and drives off without paying, or when someone has a meal in a restaurant and leaves without paying the bill.

■ There are three parts to the *mens rea* for this offence:

(1) Dishonesty: the test for dishonesty for this offence is the same test as that used in the offence of *theft* (*R* v *Ghosh, 1982*).

(2) Knowledge that payment is required (e.g. payment for a taxi ride is expected at the end of the journey — *R* v *Aziz*, 1993).

(3) Intent to avoid payment: the defendant must intend to avoid payment permanently. If the defendant claims that he or she was intending to pay at a later date, it is up to the *jury* to decide if it believes him or her (*R* v *Allen*, 1985).

■ This is an *either-way offence* with a maximum sentence of 2 years' imprisonment.

■ *TIP* This offence is different from theft, as the defendant forms the *mens rea* after he or she has obtained ownership of the *property*.

malice: (*private nuisance*) a *nuisance* committed on purpose to annoy the *claimant*.

■ If a nuisance is caused for malicious reasons, the claim is more likely to succeed.

■ *e.g.* In *Christie* v *Davey* (1893), the claimant gave music lessons and often had musical parties at his house. The *defendant* lived in the adjoining semidetached property and would deliberately bang on the wall, shout and scream to interrupt them. The claimant got an *injunction* to stop the defendant making such noises.

malice aforethought: the *mens rea* of *murder*.

manifesto promises: proposals for new laws made by political parties in the run up to a general election.

■ *e.g.* The Labour party's manifesto in 1997 promised reforms to the *House of Lords*.

manslaughter: an unlawful killing where the *defendant* does not have the required *mens rea* for *murder* (leading to a charge of *involuntary manslaughter*), or the defendant has been charged with murder and successfully pleads one of the three partial defences of *provocation, diminished responsibility* or *suicide pact* (leading to a charge of *voluntary manslaughter*).

■ The Law Commission has proposed changes to the current types of manslaughter. Voluntary manslaughter would be classed as *second-degree murder* and involuntary manslaughter would be defined as manslaughter.

■ The proposed new definition of manslaughter would encompass:
- where death was caused by a criminal act intended to cause injury, or where the offender was aware that the criminal act involved a serious risk of causing injury; or
- where there was gross negligence as to causing death.

***mansuetae naturae*:** a non-dangerous species of animal.

■ This is defined in s.2(2) of the *Animals Act 1971*:

> Where damage is caused by an animal which does not belong to a dangerous species, a keeper of the animal is liable for the damage…if:
>
> (a) the damage is a kind which the animal, unless restrained, was likely to cause or which, if caused by the animal, was likely to be severe; and
>
> (b) the likelihood of the damage or of its being severe was due to characteristics of the animal which are not normally so found in animals of the same species or are not normally found except at particular times or in particular circumstances; and
>
> (c) those characteristics were known to that keeper or were at any time known to a person who at that time had charge of the animal as that keeper's servant or, where that keeper is the head of a household, were known to another keeper of the animal who is a member of that household and under the age of sixteen

■ This lengthy definition requires the *claimant* to prove three things:

(1) *Damage* was likely to be caused, or was likely to be severe.

(2) The likelihood of the damage being caused or being severe was due to a characteristic of the animal in question (which is not usually common to that species or is only common at certain times).

(3) The characteristics were known to the *keeper.*

Master of the Rolls: the *judge* who is in charge of civil matters in the *Court of Appeal* and is president of its Civil Division.

■ The Master of the Rolls authorises *solicitors* to practise and deals with their professional rules. He or she is also consulted on any relevant matters, including practice and procedure in the civil justice system as a whole.

■ *e.g.* During *Lord Woolf's* term as Master of the Rolls, he developed the *Civil Procedure Rules 1999* that led to the *three-track system* now used by the civil courts.

***McFarlane v EE Caledonia Ltd* (1994)** (*psychiatric injury — rescuers*): the *claimant* witnessed an explosion on an oil rig and helped some of the wounded. His claim in psychiatric injury was unsuccessful as the court believed that he was not in any danger himself and was merely a bystander.

■ Bystanders cannot claim as *primary victims,* rescuers or *secondary victims* unless 'the circumstances of a catastrophe occurring very close to him were particularly horrific' (Lord Keith in *Alcock* v *Chief Constable of South Yorkshire, 1991*).

McKenzie friend: a person who is not legally qualified but who is allowed to attend court and help a person with his or her case.

***McLoughlin v O'Brian* (1983)** (*negligence — duty of care* and *psychiatric injury*): the *claimant* was able to claim *compensation* for *nervous shock* from the lorry driver who had caused an accident that had seriously injured her family. There was an obvious proximity between the lorry driver and the claimant's family, but the court held that there was also proximity between the lorry driver and the claimant. She had not witnessed the accident but she had seen her family at the hospital.

media influence: newspapers and television may try to pressurise the *government* to change the law.

■ *e.g.* The *News of the World* newspaper started a campaign after the murder of 8-year-old Sarah Payne by a child sex offender in 2000. It wanted the government to change the law so that paedophiles would be 'named and shamed'. This media campaign had a lot of backing from the public, yet the government was reluctant to change the existing law. It did, however, lead to a small change in the law.

mediation: a type of *alternative dispute resolution* where an impartial go-between speaks separately to both parties to try to find areas of agreement.

■ The mediator may suggest a solution to the dispute.

■ This form of alternative dispute resolution is useful only if the parties are willing to cooperate. The mediator may meet each party separately. Mediation is used in family disputes and may be appropriate in divorce cases (Family Law Act 1996).

There are now organisations that provide mediation services, e.g. the Family Mediators' Association and the UK College of Family Mediators.

member state: a country that is a member of the *European Union*.

mens rea: Latin for 'guilty mind'.

■ It concerns the mind-set of the defendant when the *actus reus* was committed.

■ Most crimes are fault-based and require the *defendant* to have both the *actus reus* and the *mens rea* to be criminally liable. There are a few crimes that do not require a *mens rea*, and these are known as *strict liability*.

■ There are several types of *mens rea*, and different crimes have different *mens rea* requirements. To be liable for *theft*, for example, the defendant must have acted dishonestly with the *intention to permanently deprive* the owner of his or her *property*. For *murder*, the defendant must have intended to kill or cause really serious harm.

■ *TIP* The two most commonly required types of *mens rea* are *intention* and *recklessness*.

MEP: a member of the *European Parliament*.

■ MEPs are elected every 5 years in their *member states* and are allocated seats in proportion to the population of their country. The MEPs may join one of the political parties or remain independent, and they elect a president.

mischief rule (of *statutory interpretation*)**:** allows a *judge* to ignore the wording of an *Act of Parliament* in order to reach the desired outcome in a case.

■ This rule gives judges the most flexibility when deciding what 'mischief' *Parliament* intended to stop.

■ The mischief rule was established in *Heydon's Case (1584)*. When using this rule, a judge should consider what the *common law* was before the Act was passed, what the problem was with that law, and what *remedy* Parliament was trying to provide.

■ *e.g.* The mischief rule was used in *Smith* v *Hughes (1960)*. (Also see the *purposive approach*.)

misrepresentation: a false statement made while a *contract* is being formed.

■ This may be done by mistake, negligently or fraudulently (Misrepresentation Act 1967).

mitigating factors: the court will take these into account, and they may mean that the offender receives a more lenient sentence.

■ *e.g.* Mitigating factors can include the offender's previous good character, personal circumstances and the fact that he or she has shown remorse. A prompt guilty plea can reduce the sentence by up to 20%. Other mitigating factors include: assisting the police; the fact that the offence was committed on the spur of the moment rather than being premeditated; the fact that the offender was provoked; or an attempt by the offender to compensate the victim.

■ *Aggravating factors* may increase the offender's sentence.

mode of trial hearing: a hearing that decides whether an *either-way offence* should be tried at the *Magistrates' Court* or be committed to *Crown Court*.

■ If the *defendant* pleads guilty and the Magistrates' Court accepts *jurisdiction*, it will convict the defendant and sentence him or her under s.17(a) of the Magistrates' Courts Act 1980. If the *magistrates* wish the defendant to receive a longer sentence than they have the power to give, they will commit the case to the Crown Court for sentencing under s.3 of the Powers of Criminal Courts (Sentencing) Act 2000.

■ If the defendant pleads not guilty and the magistrates believe a summary trial is more suitable, they will explain this to the defendant under s.20 of the Magistrates' Courts Act 1980. If the defendant consents to a summary trial, a date will be set. If the defendant does not wish to have the case tried summarily, the case will be sent to Crown Court under s.51 of the Crime and Disorder Act 1988.

Montesquieu: the French political thinker who put forward a theory known as the *separation of powers*.

■ His theory states that power should not be in the hands of just one person or group.

Mullin **v** *Richards* **(1998)** (*negligence — breach of duty*)**:** two 15-year-old schoolgirls were having a 'sword fight' with plastic rulers. One ruler snapped, and a piece of plastic went into the *claimant's* eye. The *defendant* had not breached her duty, as nobody had realised that this behaviour was potentially dangerous.

■ Although the test of foreseeability in negligence is objective, the defendant was a child, so the question for the *judge* was not whether the actions of the defendant were such as an ordinarily prudent and reasonable adult in the defendant's situation would have realised gave rise to a risk of injury, but whether an ordinarily prudent and reasonable child of the same age as the defendant in the defendant's situation would have realised as much.

multiplicand: see *compensatory damages*.

multiplier: see *compensatory damages*.

multi-track: trials held at the *County Court* or *High Court* involving cases worth more than £15,000 (over £50,000 for personal injury).

■ The allocation of an appropriate court usually depends on the amount being claimed and/or the complexity of the law involved in the case.

murder: an unlawful killing with *malice aforethought*.

■ Murder is a *common law* offence (see *Coke's definition of murder*).

■ The *actus reus* of murder is an 'unlawful killing'. Certain defences may make a killing lawful, e.g. *self-defence*.

■ Murder is a *result crime*. The *defendant's actus reus* must have been the cause of the victim's death. The prosecution must prove the rules of *factual causation* and *legal causation*.

■ The *mens rea* of murder is malice aforethought. The defendant must either intend to kill or intend to cause *grievous bodily harm*. *Intention* to kill is referred to as *express malice* and intention to cause grievous bodily harm as *implied malice*.

■ *TIP* The phrase 'malice aforethought' is misleading, since neither 'malice' (meaning an ill will) nor 'aforethought' (meaning premeditation) is necessary. The person who acts on the spur of the moment or the doctor who carries out *euthanasia* is equally guilty as the person who kills in cold blood.

'Murder, Manslaughter and Infanticide' (28 November 2006): *Law Commission* report that recommended that the current law of *homicide* be replaced with offences of *first-degree murder, second-degree murder* and *manslaughter*.

natural law theory: the idea that law should strongly reflect morality.

■ Natural law is seen as a 'higher law' from God (according to St Thomas Aquinas) or the foundations of human society. The theory maintains that any laws made by society that do not reflect this 'higher law' should not be obeyed.

■ *e.g.* Professor Lon Fuller defined the perfect legal system as having eight requirements: generality, promulgation, non-retroactivity, clarity, consistency, realism, constancy and congruence.

necessity: a defence that is similar to *duress of circumstances* and was not considered to exist until the case of *Re A (2000)*.

■ The test for necessity requires that an act was necessary to avoid inevitable evil, that no more was done than was necessary and that the evil inflicted was not disproportionate to the evil avoided.

■ The case of *R* v *Dudley and Stephens* (1884) did not allow the defence of necessity for *murder*. In this case, four sailors were shipwrecked and had been floating miles from land for 20 days. They killed and ate the cabin boy, who had become unconscious. Their charge of murder was upheld and the defence of necessity (the fact that they would have died if they had not eaten the victim) was not allowed.

■ The later case of *Southwark London Borough Council* v *Williams* (1971) also did not allow the defence of necessity, as Lord Denning was concerned that people would use the defence too much, e.g. by claiming if they were hungry it would be necessary for them to steal food.

necessity (*trespass to land*): defence allowing the *defendant* to *trespass* if there is an emergency, such as someone in need of help or a fire that needs to be extinguished (*Rigby* v *Chief Constable of Northamptonshire,* 1985).

■ The defence of necessity was used successfully in the *Saltpetre Case* (1606), when the defendant trespassed on the *claimant's land* to defend the realm.

■ *TIP* The use of this defence today is allowed only when there is no reasonable alternative available to the defendant.

negative resolution procedure: a vote taken by *Parliament* to cancel a piece of *delegated legislation*. This must happen within 40 days if an MP puts forward a motion to annul.

negligence: a *tort* defined by Alderson LJ in *Blyth* v *Birmingham Waterworks Co.* (1856):

> Negligence is the omission to do something which a reasonable man, guided upon those considerations which ordinarily regulate the conduct of human affairs, would do, or doing something which a prudent and reasonable man would not do.

■ Negligence is a fault-based tort. The *claimant* must prove a *duty of care*, a *breach of that duty* by the *defendant* and *damage* caused by that breach.

■ The law of negligence usually involves claims for personal injury or damage to *property*. However, there are two types of claims that the courts have been reluctant to allow: *psychiatric injury* and *pure economic loss*. These require the claimant to prove more than the normal test for a duty of care. A defendant will not always be liable for such claims, unless the extra requirements have been proved.

negligent misstatement (*negligence — pure economic loss*)**:** one of the ways in which pure economic loss can arise. It allows liability for advice that was negligently given and resulted in the *claimant* losing money.

■ Such liability was not allowed until the landmark case of *Hedley Byrne and Co. Ltd* v *Heller and Partners (1964)*.

negotiation: a type of *alternative dispute resolution* where the parties discuss the dispute between themselves in the hope of reaching an agreement.

■ This can be done with or without a *lawyer* being present.

neighbour principle: a principle developed by Lord Atkin in *Donoghue* v *Stevenson (1932)*.

■ The principle considers the question 'who in law is my neighbour?', to which Lord Atkin responded:

> …persons who are so closely and directly affected by my act that I ought reasonably to have had them in contemplation as being so affected, when I am directing my mind to the acts or omissions which are called in question.

nervous shock: see *psychiatric injury*.

***Nettleship* v *Weston* (1971)** (*negligence — breach of duty*)**:** the *defendant* was receiving driving lessons from her neighbour. She crashed and the *claimant* injured his leg. The court decided that the *standard of care* expected of a motorist was that of the ordinary reasonable driver, and it was assumed that such a driver would have passed his or her driving test. It did not matter that the defendant was a learner, as she had fallen below the standard of care expected.

non-fatal offences against the person: the criminal offences of *assault, battery, actual bodily harm* and *grievous bodily harm*.

■ Assault and battery are *common law offences* (although the sentences are defined in the *Criminal Justice Act 1988*), and actual bodily harm and grievous bodily harm are defined in the *Offences Against the Person Act 1861*.

n

- There are two types of grievous bodily harm (s.20 and s.18 of the Offences Against the Person Act 1861).
- ***TIP*** These non-fatal offences are widely criticised. Proposals for reform are contained in the *Law Commission* reports *'Offences Against the Person and General Principles' (1993)* and *'Violence: Reforming the Offences Against the Person Act 1861'*.

non-insane automatism: the *defendant* commits a crime as a result of a reflex action caused by an *external factor* such as hypoglycaemic diabetes (see *R* v *Quick, 1973*) or a reaction to a traumatic event (see *R* v *T, 1990*).

- Other examples of external factors include a blow to the head causing concussion, being stung by a bee (a famous example is *Hill* v *Baxter*, 1958), being given anaesthetic, a reflex action, being hypnotised, and suffering from severe shock or post-traumatic stress disorder.
- The defendant must show that there was a complete loss of voluntary control in order to rely on the defence of non-insane automatism.
- A successful plea of non-insane automatism will result in a full acquittal.
- ***TIP*** The key difference between *insanity* and non-insane automatism is the presence of an external factor.

non-pecuniary loss: see *compensatory damages*.

noscitur a sociis (a Latin term used in *statutory interpretation*)**:** a note stating that a word draws meanings from the other words around it.

- ***e.g.*** In *London Borough of Bromley* v *Greater London Council*, Lord Denning used the legal interpretation of the word 'economic', as it was in keeping with the rest of the *Act of Parliament*.

novus actus interveniens (*negligence — damage*)**:** a new intervening act.

- An intervening act could mean that the original *defendant* is no longer responsible for the *claimant's* injuries, e.g. the unexpected actions of a third person or of the claimant will break the *chain of causation* (see *Baker v Willoughby, 1970*).

no win, no fee: see *conditional fee agreement*.

nuisance: an activity or state of affairs that interferes with an individual's right to use and enjoy his or her *land*.

- There are three types of nuisance: *private nuisance, public nuisance* and *statutory nuisance*.
- Nuisance is a land-based tort (see *Hunter* v *Canary Wharf Ltd and London Docklands Development Corporation, 1995*).

obiter dicta (*judicial precedent*)**:** a Latin term meaning 'other things said by the way'.

■ This is not a *binding precedent*, although other *judges* may be persuaded by it (see *persuasive precedent*).

objective test: the court decides liability based on the concept of the '*ordinary reasonable man*'.

■ In a criminal case, the 'ordinary reasonable man' test is usually decided by the *jury*. In a civil case, the *judge* will decide according to what he or she believes the ordinary reasonable man would foresee as the consequences of his actions.

■ The objective test is used extensively in civil law. It is rarely used in criminal law, which tends to use a *subjective test* to decide liability.

obligation to use property in a particular way (*theft*)**:** defined in s.5(3) of the *Theft Act 1968* as:

> Where a person received property from or on account of another, and is under an obligation to the other to retain and deal with the property or its proceeds in a particular way, the property or proceeds shall be regarded (as against him) as belonging to the other.

■ This subsection is designed to cover situations where money is given to someone for a particular purpose. Even though ownership of the *property* has passed to the *defendant*, it will be regarded as theft if the defendant uses it for some other purpose.

oblique intention (also known as 'indirect intention')**:** the *defendant* did not necessarily intend the result or want it to occur, but foresaw it to a point of virtual certainty and was determined to carry on anyway.

■ *e.g.* A terrorist blows up a plane in order to kill one of the passengers. The terrorist may claim that he or she did not want to kill any passengers other than the intended target, but by blowing up a plane, it is virtually certain that all the passengers will be killed. The defendant could therefore be said to have intended their deaths if he or she knew that they were virtually certain to occur and, despite recognising this, he or she was determined to continue.

■ See *R v Moloney (1985)*, *R v Nedrick (1986)* and *R v Woollin (1998)*.

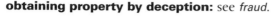

obtaining property by deception: see *fraud*.

obtaining services by deception: s.1 of the *Theft Act 1978* has now been replaced by s.11 Fraud Act 2006. It is now defined as *obtaining services dishonestly*.

obtaining services dishonestly: replaces the crime of obtaining services by deception. The elements of the offence are defined in s.11 Fraud Act 2006:

■ The *actus reus* requires obtaining services for which payment is, or will become due, and failing to pay in whole or in part.

■ The *mens rea* requires knowing that the services are to be paid for, or knowing that they might have to be paid for, with the dishonest intent to avoid payment in whole or in part.

occupier (*occupiers' liability*): the person who has some degree of control over the *premises* or *land*.

occupiers' liability: the duty owed by those who occupy *land* (and *premises* upon it) to those who enter onto it.

■ Occupiers of land and premises upon it must ensure that they discharge their duties regarding the safety of those who come onto their land.

■ The *Occupiers' Liability Act 1957* applies to lawful *visitors* or those with *express permission* or *implied permission* to enter onto the land. The *Occupiers' Liability Act 1984* applies to *trespassers*.

■ The occupier need not necessarily be the owner of the land or premises but may instead be a tenant or an *independent contractor* employed to carry out work.

■ *TIP* There may be more than one occupier at the same time, e.g. *Wheat v E. Lacon and Co.* (1966).

Occupiers' Liability Act 1957: section 2(1) states that an *occupier* of *premises* owes a common *duty of care* to lawful *visitors* to those premises. Section 2(2) defines the common duty of care as:

> The duty to take such care as in all the circumstances of the case is reasonable to see that the visitor will be reasonably safe in using the premises for the purposes for which he is invited or permitted by the occupier to be there.

■ The *standard of care* expected is the same as that in *negligence,* so the occupier need only protect the visitor from foreseeable risks.

■ An occupier will be liable for personal injury and *damage* to *property* under this Act.

■ The Act has specific rules regarding *children, persons exercising a calling* and *independent contractors*.

Occupiers' Liability Act 1984 (*occupiers' liability*): governs an *occupier's duty of care* to a *trespasser* in certain circumstances.

■ The duty is owed only if the conditions in s.1(3) of the Act are satisfied:

> An occupier of premises owes a duty to another (not being his visitor)…if:
> (a) he is aware of the danger or has reasonable grounds to believe that it exists;

(b) he knows or has reasonable grounds to believe that the other is in the vicinity of the danger concerned or that he may come into the vicinity of the danger; and

(c) the risk is one against which, in all the circumstances of the case, he may reasonably be expected to offer the other some protection.

■ Under s.1(4), the duty is 'to take such care as is reasonable in all the circumstances of the case to see that the trespasser does not suffer injury on the premises by reason of the danger concerned'. This is a question of fact in each case, and the court will consider such things as the likelihood of harm, the potential seriousness of any injury and how practical it was to take precautions against such harm occurring.

■ The occupier may have the defence of *volenti non fit injuria*, or the occupier's duty may be discharged by displaying *warning signs*.

■ *TIP* Unlike the *Occupiers' Liability Act 1957*, the Occupiers' Liability Act 1984 does not cover *damage* to *property* and an occupier is liable only for personal injury.

Offences Against the Person Act 1861: contains the definitions of *actual bodily harm* and *grievous bodily harm*.

■ Section 47 defines actual bodily harm as 'any assault occasioning actual bodily harm'.

■ Section 20 defines grievous bodily harm:

Whosoever shall unlawfully and maliciously wound or inflict any grievous bodily harm upon any other person either with or without any weapon or instrument shall be guilty of an offence triable either way and being convicted thereof shall be liable to imprisonment for 5 years.

■ Section 18 also defines grievous bodily harm:

Whosoever shall unlawfully and maliciously by any means whatsoever wound or cause any grievous bodily harm to any person, with intent to do some grievous bodily harm to any person, or with intent to resist or prevent the lawful apprehension or detainer of any person, shall be guilty of an offence triable only on indictment, and being convicted thereof shall be liable to imprisonment for life.

'Offences Against the Person and General Principles' (1993): this *Law Commission* report criticised the current *non-fatal offences*.

■ The report's main criticisms of the current law were of its complicated, obscure and old-fashioned language; complicated and technical structure; and complete unintelligibility to *lay people*.

■ The Law Commission also produced the Draft Criminal Law Bill that redefined the offences. The recommendations of this report have never been adopted.

■ See *Violence: Reforming the Offences Against the Person Act 1861* for the proposed new non-fatal offences.

offer: a proposal that if accepted constitutes a legally binding *contract*.

■ The *offeror* uses words or conduct to the *offeree* that express a willingness to make a contract.

■ In *Carlill* v *Carbolic Smoke Ball Co.* (1893), the wording of an advert indicated that the company was making a valid offer when it promised to pay £100 to anyone who used one of its products and still caught influenza. Mrs Carlill used the smoke ball and contracted influenza. The court decided that the advert was an offer and, by carrying out the conditions of the offer, Mrs Carlill had accepted it.

■ An offer may be withdrawn at any time before it is accepted. If the offer was made in an advertisement, a similar advertisement withdrawing the offer will suffice. If the withdrawal is made by post, it becomes effective only when it has been received.

offeree: the person who receives an offer in a *contract*.

offeror: the person who makes the offer in a *contract*.

omission: a failure to act.

■ In criminal law, a person is not usually liable for his or her omissions, e.g. there is no duty imposed on a passer-by to help a person drowning in a river.

■ A person will be found criminally liable for an omission only when he or she is under a duty to act and chooses to do nothing. This duty to act includes: *special relationship, professional duty to act, contractual duty to act, voluntary assumption of responsibility* and *creator of a dangerous situation*.

one transaction: see *contemporaneity*.

Orders in Council: laws passed by the *Privy Council*.

■ Orders in Council are a type of *delegated legislation*.

■ The Privy Council is a group of senior politicians who are allowed to make law without the need for the whole of *Parliament* to be sitting. They have the power to pass laws in times of emergency, with the permission of the queen under the Emergency Powers Act 1920. They may do this in wartime.

'ordinary reasonable man': see *objective test*.

'ordinary reasonable man' would have been provoked (*provocation*)**:** the *jury* must decide whether a reasonable person would have acted in the same way as the *defendant*.

■ This is the third requirement for proving the partial defence of provocation.

■ This *objective test* limits the defence and ensures that the defendant's response was not completely out of proportion to the provocation. The jury will take into account the defendant's age and sex when considering whether the 'ordinary reasonable man' would have been provoked.

■ *e.g.* In *DPP* v *Camplin (1978)*, the jury took into account the fact that the defendant was a 15-year-old boy.

■ *TIP* Other characteristics were also taken into account until the case of *Attorney General for Jersey* v *Holley (2005)*, which decided that the law should return to considering age and sex only. This decision has since been confirmed by the *Court of Appeal* in *R* v *Mohammed (2005)*; *R* v *James* and *R* v *Karimi (2006)*.

overrule (of *judicial precedent*)**:** to change the law decided in a previous case.

■ A superior court may overrule the decision of a court below it and, therefore, change the law. The *House of Lords* can use the *Practice Statement 1966* to overrule one of its earlier cases.

***Oxford* v *Moss* (1979)** (*theft*)**:** a student who took an exam paper, read the questions and then returned it could not be charged with theft of the information on the paper. This is because confidential information is not regarded as *property*. If he had kept the exam paper, this would have been theft of the paper itself. This happened in *R* v *Akbar* (2002), when a teacher was convicted of theft when she took exam papers and gave them to her students.

PACE: see *Police and Criminal Evidence Act 1984.*

***Page v Smith* (1995)** (*psychiatric injury — primary victim*)**:** the *claimant* was involved in a car accident caused by the *defendant's negligence.* The claimant was not physically injured but the shock aggravated an existing illness (chronic fatigue syndrome). His claim was successful. The court stated that a primary victim would be successful in his or her claim if physical injury is foreseeable.

■ *TIP* This case highlights a difference between primary victims and *secondary victims.* The test for foreseeability for primary victims requires that it is foreseeable that the victim would suffer psychiatric injury. Secondary victims, however, can claim only if it is foreseeable that a person of normal fortitude would suffer psychiatric injury.

palpably wrong medical treatment (*legal causation*)**:** if the victim of a crime has received negligent medical treatment, this will not break the chain of causation unless it is 'palpably wrong' — see *R v Jordan (1956).*

■ 'Palpably' means 'plain to see'.

parent act: see *delegated legislation.*

***Paris v Stepney Borough Council* (1951)** (*negligence — breach of duty*)**:** if, to the knowledge of his or her employer, an employee is suffering from a disability which, though it does not increase the risk of an accident occurring while he or she is at work, does increase the risk of serious injury if an accident should befall him or her, that special risk of injury is a relevant consideration in determining what precautions the employer should take in fulfilment of the duty to take reasonable care for the safety of each individual employee.

■ The *claimant* was employed as a fitter in the garage of the defendant borough council. He was already blind in one eye. While he was using a hammer to remove a bolt on a vehicle, a chip of metal flew off and entered his good eye, so injuring it that he became totally blind. He was able to claim compensation from his employer for not providing him with safety goggles. The *defendant* argued that the vehicle maintenance work that was being undertaken by the claimant was not dangerous enough to require goggles. The court decided that the defendant had fallen below the standard of care required, as it owed a higher standard to an employee who was more at risk.

Parliament: the institution comprising the *House of Commons*, the *House of Lords* and the monarch. All three have a role in the *legislation* process.

Parliament Acts 1911 and 1949: special procedures that allow *legislation* to bypass the *House of Lords* without its approval.

■ These are used when the House of Lords will not agree to the passing of a *bill*.

■ They are not used regularly, as the *government* will tend to come to a compromise with the House of Lords.

■ *e.g.* The Parliament Acts were used to pass the Hunting Act 2005.

Parliamentary Counsel (*legislation*)**:** also known as parliamentary draftsmen, a group of legal experts who draft the idea for a new law in legal terminology.

■ This is done at the *drafting stage* of the *legislation process*.

parliamentary stage: the most important stage of the *legislation process*.

■ The *bill* is put before *Parliament* and must pass through seven more stages: *first reading, second reading, committee stage, report stage, third reading, House of Lords,* and *royal assent.*

■ *TIP* A bill can start its journey through Parliament in either the *House of Commons* or the *House of Lords* (with the exception of finance bills, which must start in the House of Commons).

parole: the conditional early release of an offender from *prison*.

■ If someone commits any offences while on parole, he or she will be placed back in *custody* for the remaining period of the sentence.

■ *TIP* Such offenders may be fitted with an electronic *tagging* device.

participation: the involvement of people in a crime.

■ The main offender in a crime is called the *principal offender*. If more than one person is directly responsible for a crime, they are known as joint principals.

■ An accomplice/*accessory* is involved in the commission of a crime by *aiding, abetting, counselling* or *procuring* the principal offender (*secondary participation*).

past consideration: see *consideration*.

pecuniary loss: see *compensatory damages*.

***per incuriam*:** Latin for 'through lack of care'. A decision made by the court is made *per incuriam* if it fails to apply a relevant statutory provision or ignores a *binding precedent*.

■ See *Young* v *Bristol Aeroplane (1944)*.

perjury: the criminal offence of lying under oath in court.

■ This is defined in the Perjury Act 1911.

■ See *conduct crime*.

personal property (*theft*)**:** this is the most usual type of 'other property' (s.4(1) of the *Theft Act 1968*), and includes physical objects such as a stereo.

■ See *R* v *Kelly and Lindsay (1998)*.

persons exercising a calling (*occupiers' liability*)**:** section 2(3)(b) of the Occupiers' Liability Act 1957 states that:

An occupier may expect that a person, in the exercise of his calling, will appreciate and guard against any special risks ordinarily incidental to it, so far as the occupier leaves him free to do so.'

■ Those carrying out a trade are therefore expected to take measures to avoid the risks associated with it (*Roles* v *Nathan*, 1963).

■ *e.g.* An *occupier* could expect an electrician to take precautions to avoid being electrocuted.

persuasive precedent: a previous decision that does not need to be followed, but may be helpful to a *judge* when making a decision.

■ If a judge decides to follow a past decision that was not binding, the decision is said to be persuaded.

■ *e.g.* Persuasive precedents include a decision made in a lower court that is followed in a higher court, decisions made by courts not within the English hierarchy, and the *obiter dicta* of another case.

plaintiff: the old-fashioned word for *claimant.*

plea bargaining: the defence and prosecution *lawyers* negotiate an outcome for the case.

■ *e.g.* The prosecution may offer to reduce the charge of *actual bodily harm* to *common assault* if the *defendant* pleads guilty.

■ Such bargaining means that the prosecution can secure a quicker conviction and it can be dealt with by a lower court, therefore saving money.

Police and Criminal Evidence Act 1984 (PACE): defines the powers of the police.

■ These powers include *stop and search, detention, arrest, search at the police station* and *police safeguards.*

police powers: the authority of the police to *stop and search, arrest* and detain suspected criminals.

■ The amount of power given to the police to prevent and detect crime is mainly governed by the *Police and Criminal Evidence Act 1984.*

■ *Parliament* has tried to ensure that a balance is struck between allowing the police to carry out their role effectively and protecting the rights of individuals.

police safeguards: rules that are designed to protect both individual rights and the ability of the police to carry out their role effectively.

■ These are contained in the *Police and Criminal Evidence Act 1984* and the Codes of Conduct. There are safeguards relating to *stop and search, arrest* and *detention* to protect the suspect's human rights.

■ *e.g.* Under Code C, a suspect is entitled to breaks for meals, refreshments and sleep. Interview rooms must be adequately lit, heated and ventilated, and the suspect should be able to sit down.

■ Additional safeguards are found under s.57 of PACE: if the suspect is under the age of 17, an appropriate adult must be told that the suspect is being detained and given the reasons why and the location. The appropriate adult should be asked to attend the police station and can be present during any interviews. Under Code C, this also applies to those with mental disorders or a handicap.

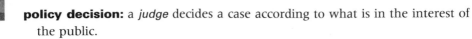

policy decision: a *judge* decides a case according to what is in the interest of the public.

■ *e.g.* Hill v *Chief Constable of West Yorkshire Police (1988).*

possession (*trespass to land*): while the *claimant* must be in possession of the *land,* he or she does not have to be the owner.

■ The possessor has immediate and exclusive possession of the land. This means that for the purposes of this *tort* a tenant, rather than the landlord, would be classed as the possessor.

postal rule: see *acceptance.*

Practice Statement 1966 (of *judicial precedent*): allows the *House of Lords* to overrule its previous decisions.

■ Before 1966 the House of Lords was bound by its own decisions. This meant that the law was certain but it could not change. In 1966, the House of Lords issued a Practice Statement, which allows it to change one of its previous decisions when 'it appears right to do so'.

■ *e.g.* The case of *Addie* v *Dumbreck* (1929) established the law that *trespassers* who get injured are not able to claim for personal injury from the *occupiers* of the *land.* This law was overruled in the case of *British Railway Board* v *Herrington* (1972) by the House of Lords using the Practice Statement 1966.

■ In criminal law, *R* v *Howe (1987)* overruled *DPP* v *Lynch* (1973) and the law that allowed *duress* to be used as a defence for *murder.* The first time the Practice Statement was used in criminal law was in the case of *R* v *Shivpuri (1986),* which overruled *Anderton* v *Ryan (1985),* changing the law regarding *attempts* to commit impossible crimes.

precedent: see *judicial precedent.*

pre-emptive strikes (*self-defence*): the *defendant* does not need to wait to be attacked before defending himself or herself.

■ In *R* v *Beckford* (1988) Lord Griffith said:

> A man about to be attacked does not have to wait for his assailant to strike the first blow or fire the first shot; circumstances may justify a pre-emptive strike.

■ If the defendant believes that he or she is at risk of an attack on his or her person or *property,* he or she may be able to make preparations in order to defend himself or herself. In Attorney General's Reference (No. 2) (1983), the defendant's shop had been attacked during riots. To try to prevent this from happening again, he made petrol bombs that he intended to use should he face attack in the future. However, there was no further attack. The defendant was charged with breaching the Explosive Substances Act 1883 by having an explosive substance in his possession. He relied on self-defence and was found not guilty.

preliminary crimes: see *inchoate offences.*

premeditation: prior resolve to do some act or commit a crime.

■ It is not necessary to prove that a crime was planned, only that it was committed. Many crimes are not premeditated, but are committed on the spur of the moment.

■ Premeditation of a crime is an *aggravating factor* that may increase the *defendant's* sentence.

premises (*occupiers' liability*): section 1(3) of the *Occupiers' Liability Act 1957* states that the term includes not only *land* and buildings, but also fixed or moveable structures such as vessels, vehicles and aircraft.

prescription (*private nuisance*): prescription is a defence where the *defendant* has been causing a nuisance continuously for 20 years, during which the *claimant* was aware of and never complained about the nuisance.

■ *e.g.* *Sturges* v *Bridgman (1879).*

pre-sentence report: a document produced by the *probation service* that outlines a *defendant's* previous convictions, mental health, and domestic and financial situation; and suggests an appropriate sentence for the crime that he or she has committed.

■ This report is used by *judges* and *magistrates* to help them decide on an appropriate sentence.

pressure group: an organisation that tries to influence the *government* to change the law.

■ *e.g.* The Snowdrop Campaign was set up after the Dunblane massacre, in which 16 children and their teacher were shot dead at a primary school in Scotland. This small group had the backing of the media and the public. It wanted to ban handguns and it influenced the Cullen Report's recommendation to change the law (see *public inquiry*).

***Pretty* v *UK* (2002)** (*consent*): the defence of consent is not available for assisted suicide/*euthanasia*.

■ Diane Pretty suffered from terminal motor neurone disease. She wished to end her life but was physically incapable of committing suicide. She wanted a guarantee from the *Director of Public Prosecutions* that her husband would not be prosecuted for assisting in her suicide since she had consented to this. The DPP refused to grant such immunity. Diane Pretty appealed to the *European Court of Human Rights* but was unsuccessful. Euthanasia remains a crime in the UK.

***prima facie*:** the Latin term for 'first appearance'.

■ This is the 'first impression' of the evidence of a case.

primary victims (*negligence — psychiatric injury*): primary victims fear for their own safety and can claim if they suffer from a medically recognised psychiatric condition, and if the physical or psychiatric harm sustained was foreseeable (see *Dulieu* v *White and Sons, 1901* and *Page* v *Smith, 1995*).

principal offender: the person directly responsible for a crime.

■ If more than one person is directly responsible for a crime, they are known as joint principals

■ If other people are involved in committing a crime, they are known as *accessories*/accomplices.

prison: see *custodial sentence*.

private bills: proposals for new laws introduced to *Parliament* by a large company, a local council or a public corporation.

■ These bills do not usually affect the whole country.

■ *e.g.* An *Act of Parliament* may need to be passed to build a new road or factory.

private members' bills: *bills* put forward by backbench MPs from any of the political parties.

■ The MP puts his or her name into a ballot at the beginning of the year and 20 names are drawn out. These MPs are then allocated time to explain their bill to the rest of the House. The *Ten-Minute Rule* does not give them much time to do this and there must be enough MPs in attendance for the vote to be counted. During the 10 minutes other MPs may waste time through false argument. This is known as *filibustering*.

■ *e.g.* A successful private members' bill led to the Murder (Abolition of the Death Penalty) Act 1965, which was proposed by Labour backbench MP Sydney Silverman.

■ *TIP* Private members' bills are usually unsuccessful, as they do not have the support of the MP's party. For example, David Alton put forward many unsuccessful private members' bills to change the abortion laws.

private nuisance: an unreasonable *interference* with a person's use or enjoyment of *land*, usually entailing civil disputes between individuals (often neighbours).

■ In order to bring a claim, the *claimant* must prove:
  (1) indirect interference with enjoyment of the land
  (2) *damage* to the claimant
  (3) the interference was unreasonable

■ Defences to claims of private nuisance include statutory authority (*Allen* v *Gulf Oil Refining Ltd,* 1981) and *prescription*. The defence of *volenti non fit injuria* (where the claimant is said to have consented to the nuisance by moving next to it) has never succeeded. The court may take into account the benefit to the public provided by the creator of the nuisance when deciding an appropriate remedy (*Adams* v *Ursell*, 1913). However, public benefit will not act as a defence in nuisance.

privity of contract: only the two parties who made a *contract* can sue each other for any breach.

■ There are exceptions to this rule, e.g. if the claim is one of *negligence* instead of *breach of contract*.

Privy Council: a group of senior politicians who have the power to pass laws in an emergency without the consent of *Parliament* (*Orders in Council*).

■ This is also the name given to the judicial role of the *House of Lords* when it decides cases involving Commonwealth countries (see *Judicial Committee of the Privy Council*).

probate: the process of establishing the validity of a *will*.

probation: a supervised period of good behaviour required of the offender after his or her release from prison.

probation order: now called a community rehabilitation order.

■ See *community sentence*.

Probation Service: a *government* organisation that supervises offenders who have been released from prison (*probation*), produces *pre-sentence reports* and provides rehabilitation for offenders who are given a *community sentence*.

pro bono (publico): legal work undertaken free of charge.

■ *Lawyers* may give free legal advice to people on low incomes.

procure (*secondary participation*): to produce by endeavour.

■ There has to be a causative link between the actions of the procurer and the offence committed by the *principal offender*.

professional duty to act (*omission*): there may be a duty for people in certain professions to act.

■ *e.g.* In *R v Dytham* (1979), a uniformed police officer watched a man being kicked to death but failed either to intervene or to summon assistance. He was guilty of misconduct in a public office, as he had neglected to protect the victim or apprehend the attackers.

promissory estoppel: a *contract* cannot be enforced if one of the parties promises the other that he or she will not enforce his or her rights under the contract.

■ See *Central London Property Trust Ltd* v *High Trees House Ltd* (1956).

property (*theft*): defined in s.4(1) of the *Theft Act 1968* to include money and all other property, whether real or personal, including things in action and other *intangible property*.

■ Personal property includes physical objects. Intangible property does not exist physically but gives the owner legal rights. It includes money in a bank account, debts, shares and intellectual property such as copyright.

■ Other guidance is found in the Theft Act 1968:

- Section 4(2) states that a person cannot steal *land* or things forming part of land and severed from it by him or by his direction.
- Section 4(3) provides that mushrooms, flowers, fruit and foliage growing wild cannot be stolen unless they are taken for 'reward or for sale or other commercial purpose'.
- Section 4(4) states that wild animals cannot be stolen unless they have been tamed or are normally kept in captivity.

■ *TIP* Electricity cannot be stolen.

property acquired by mistake (*theft*): defined in s.5(4) of the *Theft Act 1968*:

Where a person gets property by another's mistake, and is under an obligation to make restoration...an intention not to make restoration shall be regarded accordingly as an intention to deprive that person of the property or proceeds.

■ The Attorney General's Reference (No. 1 of 1983) (1985) states that if someone receives *property* by mistake and then does not give it back, this can amount

p

to theft. A legal obligation to pay it back is therefore required, rather than just a moral obligation because it is the right thing to do.

■ *e.g.* If someone is overpaid by his or her employer, there is a legal obligation to return the extra money. However, there is no legal obligation to return money paid out by mistake in a betting shop (*R* v *Gilks*, 1972).

protection of the public: ensuring that society is safe from criminals.

■ This is frequently used as a strong general justification for punishment of criminals and imprisonment in particular. It is argued that the public needs protection from dangerous criminals, and prison removes these criminals from the public domain by restricting their liberty.

provocation: a partial defence to *murder* that reduces the charge to *voluntary manslaughter*.

■ Provocation is defined in s.3 of the *Homicide Act 1957*.

■ Once there is some evidence of provocation, the *judge* must leave the matter to the *jury*. It is up to the jury to decide whether the defendant was provoked by things said or done or both together (*provocative conduct*), whether the defendant lost his or her self-control (*loss of self-control*) as a result and, finally, whether a reasonable person of the same age and sex as the defendant but with ordinary powers of self-control would have acted as the defendant did (*'ordinary reasonable man' would have been provoked*).

■ If the jury finds that the defendant was provoked, the defendant's liability will be for voluntary manslaughter rather than murder.

■ *TIP* Provocation is only a defence for the crime of murder.

provocative conduct (*provocation*)**:** things done or things said or both together, that could cause someone to lose his or her self-control.

■ This is the first requirement for proving the partial defence of provocation in *murder* cases.

■ There is no requirement that the provocative conduct be illegal. In the case of *R* v *Doughty* (1986), the court established that the crying of a young baby amounted to provocation when his father killed him, despite the fact that it is perfectly normal for babies to cry.

■ The provocation need not be directed at the *defendant* or indeed may come from someone other than the victim. In the case of *R* v *Pearson* (1992), two brothers killed their father, who had been abusing the younger of the two. The *Court of Appeal* held that the *jury* should have been told to take into account the abuse when deciding whether the older brother had been provoked, despite the fact that the abuse was not aimed at him.

proximity (*negligence*)**:** a legal connection between the *claimant* and the *defendant*.

■ This link can either be a physical connection (see *Donoghue* v *Stevenson, 1932*) or a relationship (see *McLoughlin* v *O'Brian, 1983*).

psychiatric injury (*negligence*)**:** a claim in *negligence* where the *claimant* has suffered a medically recognised condition such as severe shock.

p

■ Psychiatric injury or nervous shock is an area of restricted liability. Not all conditions will be recognised by the courts as warranting a claim. In *Tredget* v *Bexley Health Authority* (1994), profound grief suffered by the claimants after their baby died due to medical negligence was considered to be nervous shock. Lord Steyn said in *White and Others* v *Chief Constable of South Yorkshire (1999)*:

> Only recognisable psychiatric harm ranks for consideration. Where the line is to be drawn is a matter for expert psychiatric evidence.

■ *White and Others* v *Chief Constable of South Yorkshire* (1999) established three categories of claimants with psychiatric injury:

(1) Victims with physical injury and nervous shock. This type of victim can automatically claim for nervous shock along with the physical injury. There are no restrictions placed on this type of claim and the normal rules of negligence apply.

(2) *Primary victims.*

(3) *Secondary victims.*

public bill: proposals for a new law made by the *government.*

■ The contents of a public bill will affect the whole country.

public inquiry: the *government* asks a *judge* to investigate a serious event or disaster.

■ *e.g.* The Cullen Report led to the Firearms (Amendment) Act 1997, which banned handguns after the Dunblane disaster.

public nuisance: unreasonable interference affecting a group or class of people.

■ It may constitute a criminal offence and be prosecuted by the *Attorney General,* or it can be a civil claim.

■ Public nuisance differs from *private nuisance* as it can easily occur from a one-off event and is not land-based (i.e. the *claimant* does not require an interest in *land* and the *nuisance* itself does not need to arise from the *defendant's* use of land). A common claim for public nuisance arises when people are affected while using the highway.

■ A claimant who suffers more damage than other people affected by the public nuisance can make a claim for *special damage* and sue the defendant separately (*Castle* v *St Augustine's Links* (1922)).

■ Public nuisance is defined in the case of *Attorney General* v *PYA Quarries (1957).*

■ *TIP* Most public nuisances are now covered by *statutory nuisance.*

Public Order Act 1986: defines the offences of riot (s.1), violent disorder (s.2), *affray* (s.3), threatening behaviour (s.4), intentional harassment, alarm or distress (s.4(a)), disorderly conduct (s.5) and incitement to racial hatred (s.17–23).

pupillage: training undertaken by a student who has passed the *Bar Vocational Course* and wishes to become a *barrister.*

■ A pupil will shadow an experienced barrister for 6 months and then undertake his or her own work in the second 6 months.

p

■ *TIP* Competition for pupillages is fierce and many of those who have completed the Bar Vocational Course will not gain a pupillage.

pure economic loss (*negligence*): loss of money that cannot be directly attributable to the *defendant's* negligence.

■ There are two ways in which pure economic loss can arise: by *negligent misstatement* and by a negligent act.

■ The courts are reluctant to allow a claim in negligence for loss that is purely economic. This means that the *claimant* has lost money but not as a result of personal injury or *damage* to *property*. These types of claims are more suited to an action in *contract* law.

■ In cases involving businesses, pure economic loss is usually in the form of profits that the company has to speculate it would have made, e.g. *Spartan Steel and Alloys Ltd* v *Martin and Co. Ltd (1973)*.

■ The speculation of money that the claimant may or may not have received if the negligence had not occurred is difficult to quantify. Cardozo CJ in *Ultramares Corporation* v *Touche* (1931) called it 'liability to an indeterminate amount for an indeterminate time to an indeterminate class'.

■ Economic loss that is directly linked to physical injury or damage to property is recoverable. 'Pure' financial loss was limited to where there was a *contract* between the defendant and the claimant. However, after *Hedley Byrne and Co. Ltd* v *Heller and Partners (1964)*, it was thought that there were some instances where liability would be justified without a contract.

pure economic loss caused by a negligent act (*negligence — pure economic loss*): allows a claim to compensate for the *defendant's* negligent act where it has caused quantifiable loss.

■ The courts will not allow the *claimant* to claim for any losses that are not directly connected to the negligent act (see *Spartan Steel and Alloys Ltd* v *Martin and Co. Ltd, 1973*).

purposive approach (of *statutory interpretation*): when a *judge* looks beyond the actual words of an *Act of Parliament* to find the reason why the law was passed.

■ This is an extension of the *mischief rule,* as the judge will actively research the purpose of the Act of Parliament to decide how it should it applied in the present case. He or she will use *intrinsic aids* and *extrinsic aids* of interpretation.

■ *TIP* This is a more 'European' style of interpretation. It was used in *Royal College of Nursing* v *DHSS (1981)* to interpret the Abortion Act 1967.

QC: see *Queen's Counsel.*

qualified majority voting: a system of voting used by the *Council of Ministers* of the *European Union,* where each *member state* has a number of votes corresponding to the size of its population.

■ Although it may seem unfair for the larger countries of the European Union to have more votes, the growth in the number of members of the European Union means that it is difficult to get all of the member states to agree.

Queen's Bench Division (of the *High Court*): deals with *contract* and *tort* cases, as well as *judicial review* and *defamation.* It also has a specialist commercial court and an admiralty court.

Queen's Counsel (QC): a senior *lawyer* who deals with the most serious cases in court.

■ *Barristers* and *solicitors* may apply to become a Queen's Counsel. They can command much higher fees and often have a junior barrister to assist them.

■ Applicants pay an initial fee of £1,800 and a further £2,250 if they are successful. They complete a form giving details of their work and skills and listing several referees who are familiar with their work. After a selection panel has reviewed their application, candidates are interviewed.

Queen's peace: see *King's peace.*

ratio decidendi (*judicial precedent*): Latin for 'the reason for deciding'.

■ This is the binding part of a judgement and creates the law for other judges to follow (see *binding precedent*).

Re A (2000) (*necessity*): the *Court of Appeal* established the defence of necessity when it authorised the separation of conjoined twins Jodie and Mary. The court was involved in this case as the conjoined babies would not survive unless they were separated. It was known, however, that if they were separated, one of the babies would die. The parents of the babies did not want them to be separated but the court authorised the operation.

■ The test for necessity requires that an act was necessary to avoid inevitable evil, no more was done than was necessary, and the evil inflicted was not disproportionate to the evil avoided.

■ **TIP** As this case involved the *civil law*, it is only *persuasive precedent* on the *criminal law*.

Ready Mixed Concrete v Minister of Pensions and National Insurance (1968) (*vicarious liability*): it was established in this case that a person may be classed as an *employee* if three conditions are fulfilled:

(1) The person agrees that, in consideration of a wage or other remuneration, he or she will provide his or her own work and skill in the performance of some service for his or her master.

(2) He or she agrees, expressly or impliedly, that in the performance of that service he or she will be subject to the other's control in a sufficient degree to make that other master.

(3) The other provisions of the *contract* are consistent with its being a contract of service.

■ **e.g.** Conditions inconsistent with a contract of service may include, for example, the ability to hire your own employees, the requirement that you provide your own tools and materials, or the fact that you pay your own tax and national insurance. These would all indicate that someone was an *independent contractor*.

real property (*theft*): this means *land*, and is referred to in s.4(2) of the *Theft Act 1968*.

- There are three main exceptions to s.4(2):
  (1) when someone is trusted to sell or dispose of the land or anything on it and he or she breaches that confidence (e.g. the trustee benefits from the sale of the land)
  (2) when someone appropriates from land anything by severing, causing it to be severed or taking it after it has been severed (this includes taking crops, soil, bricks etc. from another person's property)
  (3) when a tenant takes something from land that is let to him or her (e.g. if a person who is renting a house takes some of the furniture when he or she moves out).

reasonable force (*self-defence*)**:** what is considered reasonable force in self-defence is a matter for the *jury* to decide in each case (see *R* v *Martin, 2002*).

- The jury must take various factors into account, including the threat of harm, the urgency of the situation and any other options that were available to the *defendant*.
- In *R* v *Palmer* (1971), it was held that a defendant did not have to 'weigh to a nicety the exact measure of his defensive action'. The jury must consider the fact that the defendant was acting in the heat of the moment and, as long as the defendant did only what he or she honestly thought was required, this will be evidence that the force used was reasonable.
- *TIP* A lower degree of force is expected if the defendant is protecting *property* rather than people.

recidivist: a repeat offender.

reckless manslaughter (*involuntary manslaughter*)**:** a reckless unlawful killing.

- There was some confusion after the ruling in *R* v *Adomako (1995)* as to whether reckless manslaughter still existed. In this case, the *House of Lords* stated that there was no need to have three types of *involuntary manslaughter* and it abolished objective reckless manslaughter. However, the *Court of Appeal* in *R* v *Lidar (1999)* allowed the trial *judge* to let the *jury* convict using subjective reckless manslaughter. It decided that this was not a separate type of involuntary manslaughter, but instead just an aspect of *gross negligence manslaughter*.

recklessness (*mens rea*)**:** an unjustifiable risk taken by the *defendant*.

- Recklessness was defined in the case of *R* v *Cunningham (1957)*. It is established using a *subjective test* and the *defendant* must recognise the risk that he or she is running.
- There were previously two different types of recklessness: subjective recklessness and objective recklessness. However, the objective form is now extinct following the case of *R* v *G and Another (2003)*.

Recorder: a part-time *judge* who may sit in both the *Crown Court* and *County Court*.

- Recorders are appointed by the queen, on the recommendation of the *Lord Chancellor*.

■ The statutory qualification for appointment as a Recorder is a 10-year Crown Court or 10-year County Court qualification.

referral order (*young offender*)**:** an order that requires a young offender to attend a Youth Offender Panel.

■ The young offender, his or her parents, the panel and sometimes the victim, all agree upon a contract aimed at repairing the damage that the offending has caused and minimising the risk of re-offending.

regulation: a type of *European Union* law.

■ Regulations state specifically what the *member state's* law should be. They are directly applicable and have a vertical and horizontal *direct effect* (see *Leonesio v Italian Ministry of Agriculture, 1973*).

regulatory offence (*strict liability*)**:** a crime that is not considered to be morally wrong.

■ *e.g.* Food regulations are much easier to enforce because the penalties are small and the requirement to prove *mens rea* has been removed (e.g. *Smedleys v Breed*, 1974).

rehabilitation: helping an offender to solve the issues that lie behind his or her criminal behaviour. The treatment is aimed at improving an offender's character or behaviour with the goal of reintegrating the offender into society.

■ The intention is that if the problems are solved then the offender will avoid committing further offences.

■ *e.g.* A drug addict who steals to fund his or her habit may be helped to overcome the addiction, thereby removing the need to steal in future.

remand: placing the *defendant* in *custody* pending trial.

■ A defendant will be remanded in custody if the *Magistrates' Court* will not grant *bail*.

remedies: used in *civil law* to solve the dispute between the parties involved.

■ The two main remedies that the court may order are *damages* or an *injunction*.

reparation: 'making amends' for a crime.

■ An offender may be required to attempt to 'repair' the damage caused by his or her offence, usually by carrying out work in the community or by paying financial compensation. This encourages offenders to accept responsibility for their crimes.

reparation order (*young offender*)**:** a type of *community sentence* where offenders must try to repair the harm caused by their offence.

■ If the victim agrees, he or she may have direct contact with the offender. Otherwise, the offender repays the community as a whole — usually by carrying out work such as cleaning graffiti.

report stage (of the *legislation process*)**:** where the *standing committee* reports back to the House with any proposals for changes to the *bill*.

■ Each change is debated and voted on by the House. This is followed by the *third reading*.

■ **TIP** If there are no proposed changes, this stage does not occur.

rerum natura (*Coke's definition of murder*): 'any reasonable creature in *rerum natura*' is understood to be a person who is born and not dead.

■ Generally, the beginning of life is taken to be when a baby has an existence independent of its mother. However, see *Attorney General's Reference No. 3 (1994)*. The end of life can be difficult to determine.

■ There is no legal definition, but generally brain-stem death is accepted as signalling the end of life (see *R v Malcherek, R v Steel, 1981*).

rescuers (suffering *psychiatric injury*): rescuers who suffer psychiatric injury at the scene of an accident can claim for compensation only if they were in personal danger.

■ A fireman successfully claimed for post-traumatic stress disorder after his involvement in the rescue operation during the fire at King's Cross Station (*Hale v London Underground*, 1992). A person who helped rescue people involved in the Lewisham train disaster successfully claimed for psychiatric injury in *Chadwick v British Transport Commission* (1967). However, the *claimant* in *McFarlane v EE Caledonia Ltd (1994)* was unsuccessful.

■ According to the decision in *White and Others v Chief Constable of South Yorkshire (1999)*, rescuers who were not in any personal danger should be treated the same as *secondary victims*.

res ipsa loquitur (*negligence — damage*): Latin for 'the facts speak for themselves'.

■ This principle is applied when it cannot be proved exactly what happened, but the facts show that the *defendant* must have been negligent. In *Mahon v Osborne* (1939), the claimant awoke from an operation. Someone had failed to remove cotton wool swabs from her stomach, which became infected. The hospital was negligent based on this evidence.

■ *e.g.* *Scott v London and St Katherine's Docks* (1865).

result crimes: where the *defendant's* actions caused the prohibited result.

■ *e.g.* In *murder* cases, the prosecution must prove that it was the defendant's actions that caused the death of the victim. In order to establish this, the prosecution must prove a causal link between the action and the consequence (see *causation*).

retribution: the aim of a retributive sentence is to punish the offender.

■ The phrase 'an eye for an eye, a tooth for a tooth' is often used when discussing this aim. The idea is that if a person has knowingly done wrong, he or she deserves to be punished and society expects this to happen.

■ *e.g.* In the past, the death penalty was used to punish murderers.

reverse (of *judicial precedent*): a superior court may change the outcome of a case from a lower court based on the same law.

■ *e.g.* The *Crown Court* applies the existing law and finds the *defendant* guilty, whereas the *Court of Appeal* applies the same law and finds the person not guilty.

***Rice* v *Connolly* (1966)** (*police powers*)**:** this case shows that the police may question individuals, but those individuals are entirely free to decline to answer unless arrested.

■ A member of the public was considered to be behaving suspiciously in an area where several *burglaries* had occurred. The police questioned the individual but he refused to answer. His conviction for obstructing a police officer in the execution of his duty was quashed, and it was confirmed that members of the public are not under any obligation to answer questions.

***Ricketts* v *Cox* (1982):** this case shows that there is a thin line between lawfully refusing to answer questions and obstructing the police.

■ The police asked an individual questions about an *assault*. He was hostile and used abusive language. *Magistrates* decided that he was guilty of obstruction.

right of audience: the ability to represent a client in court.

■ Traditionally, *solicitors* were only able to represent their clients in the *Magistrates' Court* and *County Court*, whereas *barristers* had full rights of audience.

■ Since the *Courts and Legal Services Act 1990*, solicitors can train to be *solicitor advocates* with greater rights of audience.

right to silence: a *defendant* does not have to answer questions at the police station or in court.

■ The defendant is innocent until proven guilty, so the *burden of proof* is on the *prosecution* to prove that the defendant was to blame.

■ This right was altered in the Criminal Justice and Public Order Act 1994. If the defendant does not answer questions, the prosecution will imply that this is a sign (but not proof) of guilt when telling the court of this silence.

■ *TIP* The police inform defendants about this right when cautioning them during the *arrest*.

riot: an offence that is committed when 12 or more people, who are present together, use or threaten unlawful violence for a common purpose.

■ Their conduct must be such that it would cause a person of reasonable firmness present at the scene to fear for his or her personal safety.

■ Riot is defined in s.1 of the *Public Order Act 1986*. This offence can be committed in public or in private, and no person of reasonable firmness needs to be present.

■ The maximum sentence for riot is 10 years' imprisonment and a *fine*.

robbery: defined in s.8 of the *Theft Act 1968*:

A person is guilty of robbery if he steals, and immediately before or at the time of doing so, he uses force on any person or puts or seeks to put any person in fear of being subjected to force.

■ The *actus reus* of robbery overlaps with that for *theft* (*appropriation* of *property belonging to another*), but has the additional requirement of *force* or threat of force on any person immediately before or at the time of stealing. See *R* v *Clouden (1987)* and *R* v *Dawson and James (1976)*.

■ The appropriation does not have to be complete, as long as the *defendant* assumes one of the rights of the owner (see *Corcoran* v *Anderton, 1980*).

■ The *mens rea* of robbery is the same as that for theft (*dishonesty* and *intention to permanently deprive*), plus intentional or reckless application of force (see *R* v *Robinson, 1977*).

Rose v Plenty (1976) (*vicarious liability*)**:** this case shows that when an act has been expressly forbidden but is done for the benefit of the employer, an employer may be vicariously liable.

■ The employers placed a notice at their depot expressly forbidding milkmen to allow children onto their vehicles. Despite this, one milkman allowed a 13-year-old boy to help him on his round. The employers were held vicariously liable when the boy was injured as a result of the negligent driving of the milkman. The *Court of Appeal* held that the milkman was doing the job that he had been employed to do for the benefit of his employers. As such, it was conduct that was in the *course of his employment*, despite the fact that he had breached the employers' express instructions.

rough horseplay (*consent*)**:** boisterous play.

■ The courts have accepted consent as a defence even to serious injury sustained during horseplay. It is thought that this is because it is an area in which the courts do not want to see criminal prosecutions.

■ *e.g.* *R* v *Jones (1986)*.

royal assent: the final stage of the *legislation process* when the queen signs the *bill*.

■ After royal assent, the bill becomes an *Act of Parliament*.

Royal College of Nursing v DHSS (1981): an example of the *purposive approach* of *statutory interpretation*.

■ The Abortion Act 1967 was written at a time when only 'registered medical practitioners' (doctors) were authorised to carry out abortions. The case questioned the legality of the involvement of nurses in the modern practice of non-surgical abortions. The *judge* found that the purpose of the *Act of Parliament* was to stop back-street abortions, not to prevent involvement from nurses.

Royal Commission: a group of independent experts who are asked by the *government* to consider a specific area of concern in the law.

■ The commissions are set up on an ad hoc basis and work part time to investigate the issue and then formulate their proposals. After their report is finished, the groups disband. These groups are usually set up when there is a problem with an existing area of law.

■ *e.g.* See the *Runciman Commission*.

rule of law: written by *Dicey*, it establishes three rules that form the basis of the UK constitution.

■ The three rules state:
  • There should be no sanction without breach (meaning no one should be punished unless he or she has been found guilty).

- All men shall be governed by the same law (meaning the law is the same for everyone and no one is above the law).
- Rights of individuals should be decided by *judges* instead of a written constitution.

Runciman Commission: a *Royal Commission*, which was set up by the *government* after the release of the Birmingham Six.

■ It investigated the failings of the criminal justice system, and recommended the creation of the Criminal Appeals Act 1995 and the establishment of the *Criminal Case Review Commission*, which considers cases where a possible miscarriage of justice has occurred.

R v *Adomako* **(1995)** (*gross negligence manslaughter*)**:** the *defendant* was an anaesthetist during the latter part of an eye operation conducted at Mayday Hospital, Croydon on 4 January 1987. Forty-five minutes into the operation, the first anaesthetist and his assistant left to attend another operation. Dr Adomako then became the anaesthetist-in-charge, although his assistant did not arrive until later. The patient died within the next 45 minutes. An oxygen tube had become disconnected from the ventilator, which the defendant failed to notice for 6 minutes. By this time, the patient had suffered a cardiac arrest and attempts to resuscitate were unsuccessful. There was conflicting evidence as to whether the defendant was actually in the room. The defendant appealed against his conviction to the Criminal Division of the *Court of Appeal*, who dismissed the appeal. The *House of Lords* unanimously dismissed a further appeal, upholding the conviction and the sentence. The leading judgement came from the then *Lord Chancellor*, Lord Mackay of Clashfern, who defined the *common law* offence of gross negligence manslaughter.

R v *Ahluwalia* **(1992)** (*provocation* and *diminished responsibility*)**:** the *defendant's* husband had abused her for many years. One evening, he threatened her with violence to take place on the next day. He then went to bed and, while he was asleep, she poured petrol over him and set it alight. She was charged with *murder* when he died as a result of his injuries. Her first appeal against conviction failed because the *Court of Appeal* took into account the delay between the provocation and her response (a *cooling-off period*). The second appeal was successfully based on the defence of diminished responsibility. It was said in that appeal, however, that a time delay did not automatically mean that the defence of provocation failed, as the defendant might still have had a sudden and temporary *loss of self-control* at the last moment.

R v *Allen* **(1872):** an example of the narrow approach of the *golden rule* of *statutory interpretation*. The wording of the *Offences Against the Person Act 1861* had to be given a different interpretation for the crime of bigamy, because the way it was written meant that the crime could never be committed.

R v *Billinghurst* **(1978)** (*consent*)**:** the defence of consent may be allowed if the victim sustains injuries that are likely to occur when playing certain sports.

■ The *defendant* punched an opponent and fractured his jaw in an off-the-ball incident during a rugby match. The defendant tried to rely on the victim's consent, arguing that rugby is a game involving physical contact to which the players are taken to consent. However, the *jury* convicted him of *grievous bodily harm* after deciding that he had gone beyond what was being consented to.

R **v** *Blaue* **(1975)** (*legal causation* — susceptibility of the victim): if some pre-existing weakness or medical condition of the victim makes the result of an attack more severe than it would be ordinarily, the *defendant* cannot argue that the *chain of causation* has been broken. This also applies to beliefs.

■ The defendant stabbed his victim after she refused to have sex with him. In hospital, the victim refused a blood transfusion on the grounds that, as she was a Jehovah's Witness, it was against her religious beliefs to undergo the procedure. Medical opinion was that she would not have died if she had had the transfusion. The defendant's conviction for *manslaughter* was upheld, despite his argument that the victim's refusal to accept treatment was unreasonable and should therefore break the chain of causation. The court took the view that the defendant had to take his victim as he found her, including any religious beliefs that she may have held.

R **v** *Brown* **(1985)** (*burglary*): the *defendant* was charged with s.9(1)(a) burglary. He was caught with the top half of his body through a broken shop window and his feet on the ground outside. He argued that he could not be said to have entered the building, as only part of his body had been inside it. However, the *Court of Appeal* upheld his conviction, saying that the critical issue was whether the entry had been effective, not substantial and effective as stated in *R* v *Collins (1973)*.

■ See *R* v *Ryan (1996)* for a more recent definition of *entry*.

R **v** *Brown and Others* **(1993)** (*consent*): the *defendants* were members of a group that engaged in sadomasochistic homosexual activities, including genital torture and branding. The acts were done in private, with the consent of everyone involved. The police found videos of the activities and the men were charged with various counts of both *actual bodily harm* and *grievous bodily harm*. The question arose as to whether the defendants could rely on the consent of the victims as a defence. The majority of the *House of Lords* decided that such activities were not conducive to the welfare of society and so declined to include them in the list of recognised exceptions to the rule that a victim cannot consent to anything beyond *common assault*. Their convictions were upheld.

■ A similar situation arose in the case of *R* v *Wilson (1996)* but the courts took a different view.

R **v** *Byrne* **(1960)** (*diminished responsibility*): the *defendant* strangled his victim in a hostel and then mutilated her body. He claimed that he was unable to control his perverted sexual desires and had acted under an irresistible impulse. The original trial *judge* directed the *jury* that diminished responsibility was not relevant in this case. The *Court of Appeal* held that the term *'abnormality of mind'* covered all aspects of the mind, including the ability to control physical acts as well as the ability to make rational decisions. Byrne's *murder* conviction was reduced to *voluntary manslaughter*.

***R v Church* (1967)** (*constructive manslaughter*): the *defendant* had an argument with a woman in the back of his van. He had been unable to satisfy her sexually and she had slapped him in the face. The defendant knocked her unconscious and, thinking she was dead, he threw her into the river to dispose of the body. She drowned in the river.

■ The *Court of Appeal* established the test for dangerousness in this case. The unlawful act must be such as 'all sober and reasonable people would inevitably recognise must subject the other person to, at least, the risk of some harm resulting therefrom, albeit not serious harm'. As this is an *objective test*, it did not matter that the defendant did not see a risk of some harm when he threw the victim into the river.

***R v Clouden* (1987)** (*robbery*): the *defendant* was charged with robbery when he wrenched a shopping bag from the victim's hand. The *Court of Appeal* held that the *force* applied to the *property* was sufficient to amount to robbery. What amounts to force should be left to the *jury* to decide.

■ *TIP* The Criminal Law Revision Committee criticised the decision in this case.

***R v Cocker* (1989)** (*provocation*): the *defendant* killed his wife, who was suffering from a terminal disease. She had asked him repeatedly to suffocate her with a pillow. At his *murder* trial, he tried to rely on her repeated requests to end her life as provocation. On appeal, his conviction was upheld, as the *Court of Appeal* did not consider that there had been a sudden and temporary *loss of self-control*.

***R v Collins* (1973)** (*burglary*): the *defendant* saw an open bedroom window. He climbed up a ladder and saw a naked girl lying asleep on the bed. He went back down the ladder and took off all of his clothes except for his socks. He then climbed back up and stood on the windowsill. The girl awoke and, thinking that Collins was her boyfriend, invited him in. They had sex, after which the girl realised he was not her boyfriend and told him to leave. He was charged with s.9(1)(a) burglary but there was a misdirection at the trial and the *Court of Appeal* quashed his conviction. The Court of Appeal stated that *entry* of the building as a *trespasser* had to be 'substantial and effective'. The fact that the defendant was standing on the windowsill meant that his entry was not substantial and effective. When he actually entered the bedroom, he was not a trespasser, as the girl had invited him in.

■ See *R v Brown (1985)* and *R v Ryan (1996)* for more recent definitions of entry.

***R v Conway* (1989)** (*duress by circumstances*): the *defendant* was in his car with a passenger when two plain-clothed policemen started running towards them. Not knowing that they were policeman, the defendant and the passenger feared that they were in immediate threat of personal injury because the passenger had been recently threatened in such a way and the defendant drove off recklessly at high speed. The *Court of Appeal* quashed the conviction for reckless driving, as the *judge* should have allowed the *jury* to consider duress by circumstances as a possible defence at the trial.

R v Cunningham **(1957)** (*recklessness*): in need of money, the *defendant* removed a gas meter from a wall in order to take the cash within it. Removing the meter allowed gas to escape and to enter the house next door, where the occupant inhaled it and became ill. Cunningham was charged with 'maliciously administering a noxious thing so as to endanger life' contrary to s.23 of the *Offences Against the Person Act 1861*. The courts were asked to consider the meaning of the word 'malicious', which they stated did not require ill will or bad feeling but should simply be taken to mean that the defendant acted either intentionally or recklessly. They went on to say that recklessness required the defendant to foresee the chance or possibility of the result occurring. Thus, in order to be found guilty, Cunningham must have realised there was a risk that, in acting as he did, the gas might escape and endanger somebody's life, and, recognising that risk, he removed the meter anyway.

■ Also see *R v G and Another (2003)*.

■ *TIP* Recklessness uses a *subjective test* and is sometimes referred to as 'Cunningham subjective recklessness'.

R v Dawson and James **(1976)** (*robbery*): one *defendant* nudged the victim in the back so that he lost his balance while the other defendant took the victim's wallet. The amount of *force* used was sufficient to be classed as a robbery. The word 'force' has been interpreted in the ordinary sense of the word. It does not require any violence.

R v Dica **(2004)** (*consent*): the defence of consent applies only if the victim was informed of the risks.

■ The *defendant* slept with two women who were unaware that he was HIV positive. The victims had not consented to the risk of HIV infection, as they had been unaware that the defendant was infected.

■ This notion of informed consent was followed in *Konzani* (2005) — another case of HIV infection. The defendant could not rely on the defence of consent, as his victims had only consented to unprotected sex and not to the risk of infection with a fatal disease.

R v Dietschmann **(2003)** (*diminished responsibility*): the *House of Lords* held that a *defendant* might be able to rely on the defence of diminished responsibility despite being intoxicated, as long as the *abnormality of mind* was still a substantial cause of the killing.

■ The defendant had been in a relationship with his aunt and suffered from depression when she died. After drinking heavily, the defendant attacked his victim as he believed he had broken his watch — a gift from his dead aunt. At his trial, the question arose as to whether the defendant could rely on the defence of diminished responsibility, despite the fact that he had been drinking. The House of Lords held that although drink could not be taken into account when considering his mental abnormality, it might have been the case that the defendant's mental abnormality and alcohol both had a part in impairing his mental responsibility. If so, it is up to the *jury* to decide whether, despite the drink, his mental abnormality substantially impaired his mental responsibility for his actions. If this is the case, the defence would still be available, despite the fact that he would not have killed had he been sober.

R v *Dyke and Munro* (2002) (*theft*): the *defendants* collected and kept money intended for a children's cancer fund. They were charged with stealing money from the public who had put the money in the tins. The *Court of Appeal* quashed their conviction. It said that the defendants should not have been charged with stealing the money from the unknown members of the public who put it into the collection tin. Instead, they should have been charged with stealing the money from the charity, as ownership of the money had passed to the charity when it had been put in the collection tin.

R v *G and Another* (2003) (*recklessness*): two children aged 11 and 12 put lit newspaper under a wheelie-bin in a yard. The bin caught fire and the fire spread to shops and other nearby buildings, causing over £1 million of damage. The boys were charged with *arson*, but at their trial they argued that they had not seen the risk that the fire might spread. The *House of Lords* applied the Cunningham test of *subjective recklessness* (see *R v Cunningham, 1957*), and since the *defendants* had not appreciated the risk, they were not guilty of arson.

R v *Geddes* (1996) (*attempts*): the *defendant* was found in the boys' toilets of a school. He ran off, leaving a rucksack containing string, tape and a knife. He was convicted of attempted *false imprisonment* but on appeal this was quashed, as, despite the fact that he clearly had the requisite intention, his actions were preparatory. He had not progressed beyond the preparatory stage, since he had not made contact with any of the boys. He had simply put himself in the position of being able to commit the offence and had not moved into the implementation stage.

R v *Ghosh* (1982) (*theft*): the *Court of Appeal* established a two-stage test for *dishonesty* in this case, which combines both an objective and a subjective element.

(1) 'A *jury* must first of all decide whether according to the ordinary standards of reasonable and honest people what was done was dishonest.' This is the objective part of the test for dishonesty. If the answer to (1) is no, then the *defendant* is not guilty of theft. If the answer to (1) is yes, number (2) must then be proved.

(2) 'If it was dishonest by those standards, then the jury must consider whether the defendant himself must have realised that what he was doing was by those standards dishonest.' This is the subjective element of the Ghosh test.

R v *Graham* (1982) (*duress*): the *Court of Appeal* established a two-part test for the defence of *duress by threats* in this case.

- The *defendant* lived with his wife and homosexual lover. His lover threatened him into killing his wife. The Court of Appeal did not regard the threats as sufficient to constitute the defence of duress.
- For duress by threats to succeed, the *jury* needs to consider the two key questions raised by Lord Lane CJ:
  (1) Was the defendant impelled to act in the belief that he or she or others would be killed or physically injured if he or she did not comply with the threats?
  (2) If so, would a sober person of reasonable firmness sharing the same characteristics as the defendant have acted in the same way?

This creates a two-part test with a subjective element (1) and an objective test (2):

- The first part of the Graham test requires the threats to be serious, unavoidable and imminent, and the duress must not be self-induced.
- The second part of the Graham test requires a sober person of reasonable firmness to have also done as the defendant did. The court will, however, take into account some of the defendant's characteristics. The jury can also take into account a defendant's physical disability or mental illness.

R v Gullefer (1987) (*attempts*): the *defendant* had placed a bet on a greyhound at a racetrack, but it soon became obvious that his choice was not going to win. The defendant ran onto the track in order to disrupt the race, so that it would be declared void and he could then retrieve his stake money from the bookmakers. The question was whether his actions could be said to be more than merely preparatory to the commission of *theft*. The *Court of Appeal* overturned his conviction for attempted theft. It said that he had not gone beyond the preparatory stages, as he still had to go to ask for his money back from the bookmakers.

R v Hardie (1984) (*involuntary intoxication*): after arguing with his girlfriend, the *defendant* took some of her Valium tablets to calm his nerves. Valium is a sedative and its usual effect is to make the person sleepy. In this case, however, it failed to have the usual effect and, while under its influence, the defendant set fire to his flat. On appeal, his conviction under the *Criminal Damage Act 1971* was overturned. The *Court of Appeal* said that since the usual effect of the drug was soporific, the defendant was not reckless in taking it if he was unaware that it would have an unexpected effect upon him.

R v Hasan (2005) (*duress*): in order to prove the defence of *duress by threats*, the threat had to be immediate or almost immediate so that the *defendant* did not have time to inform the police or to avoid committing the crime.

- The defence of duress is not available where the defendant has voluntarily associated with criminals. The defendant should have reasonably foreseen that he or she might be forced to commit crimes by threats or violence.
- The defendant was the driver for a prostitute whose boyfriend threatened him with violence if he did not commit a *burglary*. The defendant was caught and

tried to use the defence of duress by threats. The *House of Lords* did not allow the defence, as his duress was self-induced, regardless of whether he had foreseen that he might be forced to commit crimes. All that was necessary was that either the defendant foresaw or it was reasonable to foresee that he might be forced.

■ *TIP* The decision in this case has restricted a defendant's chance of proving the defence of duress. Previous cases such as *R* v *Hudson and Taylor* (1971) and *R* v *Abdul-Hussain* (1999), which were allowed the defence of duress, would probably fail since *R* v *Hasan*. In *R* v *Hudson and Taylor* (1971), the defendants were allowed the defence of duress for the offence of *perjury* when they lied in court after being threatened by one of the friends of the defendant. In *R* v *Abdul-Hussain* (1999), Iraqi fugitives were allowed the defence of duress when they hijacked an aeroplane that they flew to England.

R v *Hinks* (2000) (*theft*): the *defendant* befriended a rich man of low intelligence. She convinced him to withdraw £300 a day and put it into her bank account. The majority of the *House of Lords* held that the £60,000 she had received from the victim was an *appropriation*, regardless of it being a gift. The defendant's charge of theft was upheld.

R v *Howe* (1987) (*duress*): duress is not a defence for *murder*.

■ The *defendant* was part of a criminal gang that tortured and killed two people. Howe was the lookout for the gang and pleaded duress to the murders. His conviction was upheld by the *Court of Appeal* and the *House of Lords*, both of which decided duress should not be available for the crime of murder. This decision *overruled* the previous law that allowed the defence of duress for a getaway driver who was threatened by the IRA (*DPP for Northern Ireland* v *Lynch*, 1975).

■ The House of Lords also stated that duress should not be a defence for attempted murder. This *obiter dictum* made by the court was followed in the later case of *R* v *Gotts* (1991).

R v *Ibrams and Gregory* (1981) (*provocation*): a planned attack will not be regarded as a *loss of self-control* and the defence of provocation will fail.

■ The victim had been terrorising the defendants, who had sought but had not received protection from the police. The *defendants* made a plan to attack the victim a few days later. They planned to break his arms and legs but the victim subsequently died from injuries sustained in the attack. On appeal, their convictions for *murder* were upheld since there was no evidence of a 'sudden and temporary' loss of self-control during the pre-planned attack.

R v *Ireland*, *R* v *Burstow* (1997): these cases established that silent telephone calls, which cause *psychiatric injury*, can constitute *ABH* or even *GBH*.

R v *Jones* (1986) (*consent/rough horseplay*): the victim was thrown into the air by his classmates. He sustained a broken arm and a ruptured spleen. Despite the serious nature of his injuries, the defence of consent was allowed as the boys involved, including the victim, had treated the incident as a joke and there was no *intention* to cause injury.

R v Jones and Smith (1976) (*burglary*): the *defendant* had permission to enter his parents' house, but when he did so in the middle of the night with his friend and took two television sets, the court held that he was a *trespasser*. The *Court of Appeal* said:

> A person is a trespasser if he enters premises of another knowing that he is entering in excess of the permission that has been given to him to enter, or being reckless whether he is in excess of that permission.

R v Jordan (1956) (*legal causation* — medical treatment): medical treatment will not break the *chain of causation* unless it is 'palpably wrong'.

■ The *defendant* stabbed the victim. The victim had been recovering well until being given a large quantity of drugs to which he was allergic. The victim died 8 days later, by which time the stab wound had mainly healed. The hospital treatment was described as 'palpably wrong' and the *Court of Appeal* said that as such it broke the chain of causation. This meant that Jordan was not responsible for the death.

■ **TIP** It is rare for medical treatment to break the chain of causation, since the courts take the view that it would not have been required were it not for the conduct of the defendant (*R v Smith*, 1959 and *R v Cheshire*, 1991).

R v Kelly and Lindsay (1998) (*theft*): the *defendants* took body parts from the Royal College of Surgeons. They were found guilty of theft, even though body parts are not usually regarded as *property*.

R v Kennedy (1999) (*constructive manslaughter*): the *defendant* supplied the victim with a syringe of heroin, which the victim injected immediately before leaving. The victim died an hour later. The defendant was charged with constructive manslaughter but he appealed to the *Court of Appeal*. He argued that it was not the supply of the drug that had caused the death but the victim injecting himself, and, therefore, the self-injection had broken the *chain of causation*. The Court of Appeal upheld the conviction by making the defendant an *accomplice* to the self-injection.

■ This case raised many criticisms, as the court did not specify exactly which unlawful act caused the victim's death. The earlier case of *R v Dalby* (1982) held that supply of a drug alone could not constitute manslaughter. The Court of Appeal in *R v Dias* (2002) quashed the conviction of the defendant in a case that was similar to *R v Kennedy*. However, in *R v Rodgers* (2003) the defendant was found guilty of constructive manslaughter when he helped the victim inject himself by applying a tourniquet.

R v Kennedy (2005): Following the earlier case of *R v Kennedy (1999)*, Kennedy got a second appeal to the *Court of Appeal* in 2005. The court accepted that mere supply of drugs cannot constitute manslaughter, but it thought that Kennedy was guilty of manslaughter because he did more than merely supply.

By making up the syringe of heroin, Kennedy was 'in concert' with the victim, and therefore the unlawful act was administering a noxious substance as defined in s.23 of the *Offences Against the Person Act 1861*.

R v *Kingston* **(1994)** (*intoxication*)**:** the *defendant* was a known paedophile. A business associate set out to blackmail him and invited him round to his flat. Once there, his drink was spiked and he was taken to a room where a 15-year-old boy was asleep and told to abuse him. The defendant did so and his associate photographed the attack. The *House of Lords* upheld his conviction for indecent assault, despite the fact that his intoxication was involuntary. This was because the defendant admitted that he had intended to *assault* the boy. He was therefore guilty since he had formed the relevant *mens rea*, despite his intoxicated state.

R v *Lamb* **(1967)** (*constructive manslaughter*)**:** the *defendant* killed his best friend with a revolver. He did not have the appropriate *mens rea*, as neither of the men thought the gun would fire. The defendant was not liable for his friend's death as it was seen as an accident.

R v *Larsonneur* **(1933):** the *defendant* was a French woman who was deported from Ireland and forcibly taken to the UK. When she arrived in England, she was promptly arrested for being an illegal alien, contrary to the Aliens Order 1920. She had been found in the UK when she did not have permission to be there. She was convicted and appealed on the basis that immigration officers had taken her to the UK against her will, but the *Court of Appeal* upheld her conviction, thus making this offence a *state of affairs crime*.

R v *Latimer* **(1886)** (*transferred malice*)**:** during an argument in a pub, the *defendant* took off his belt and swung it at his intended victim. The belt hit a bystander instead, causing injury. Latimer was convicted of wounding, as the courts transferred his *intention* to hit the intended victim onto his actual victim, ensuring that he had both the *actus reus* and *mens rea* of the offence.

R v *Lidar* **(1999)** (subjective *reckless manslaughter*)**:** the *defendant* drove off with the victim hanging out of the car window. The victim was killed after falling out of the window and being run over by the defendant. The *Court of Appeal* said that there was nothing in the case of *R* v *Adomako (1995)* to suggest that subjective reckless manslaughter had been abolished. It decided that this was not a separate type of *involuntary manslaughter*, but instead just an aspect of *gross negligence manslaughter*.

R v *Malcherek, R* v *Steel* **(1981):** (*legal causation* and *rerum natura*) a doctor switching off a life-support machine will not break the *chain of causation*.

■ In Malcherek, the *defendant* stabbed his wife, who subsequently suffered irreparable brain damage from a blood clot. Doctors carried out the relevant tests and then switched off her life-support machine when it was determined that she had suffered brain death. In Steel, the defendant had attacked the victim with a large stone, causing severe head injuries. She never regained consciousness and her life-support machine was switched off. Both men were convicted of *murder* and appealed on the basis that the cause of death was the switching off of the life-support machine. As doctors will not switch off machines until tests have established brain-stem death, the *Court of Appeal* upheld both murder convictions.

■ The *judges* also considered the medical definition of death. This is said to be 'brain-stem death', i.e. death occurs when the brain stem is no longer functioning.

R v *Martin* **(1989)** (*duress by circumstances*)**:** the *defendant* drove his stepson to work, even though he was disqualified from driving. The reason he drove while disqualified was because his wife threatened to kill herself if he did not. The *Court of Appeal* established a two-stage test for duress by circumstances that is similar to the Graham test (see *R* v *Graham, 1982*). It involves a *subjective test*, in that the defendant reasonably believed that death or serious injury would result. The second part of the test is objective, in that the sober person of reasonable firmness would have done as the defendant did. The defendant was successful and his conviction was quashed.

R v *Martin* **(2002)** (*self-defence*)**:** the *defendant* was a farmer who lived on an isolated farm. One night, two burglars broke into the farmhouse and the defendant shot them, killing one and wounding the other. He was charged with *murder*. At his trial, he sought to rely on self-defence. However, this was rejected by the *jury*, as it was felt that he had used excessive force. The *Court of Appeal* eventually quashed his murder conviction on the basis of *diminished responsibility*.

R v *Matthews and Alleyne* **(2003)** (*murder*)**:** the two *defendants* robbed the victim and then pushed him off a bridge into a river, despite the victim's protestations that he was unable to swim. Both defendants claimed that they lacked the necessary *mens rea* for murder — they had not intended to kill their victim. The *judge* directed the *jury* that if the defendants appreciated that drowning was a virtual certainty then they must have had the *intention* to kill him. On appeal, it was stressed that even if the defendant does foresee death or *grievous bodily harm* as a virtual certainty, the jury may find intention but it does not have to. It is simply a rule of evidence rather than of law, and it is something that a jury may use to help it to decide whether or not the defendant had the necessary intention.

■ *TIP* This means that the definitions of intention from the cases of *R* v *Nedrick (1986)* and *R* v *Woollin (1998)* are only guidelines.

R v *Miller* **(1983)** (*omission, contemporaneity* and *criminal damage/arson*)**:** the *defendant* was a squatter in a house. One night, he fell asleep on a mattress while smoking a cigarette. He awoke to find that his cigarette had set fire to the mattress. However, he did not extinguish the flames but simply got up, moved to another room and went back to sleep, doing nothing to stop the spread of the fire. Significant *damage* was caused to the house and the defendant was convicted of criminal damage. The *House of Lords* upheld his conviction and said that on realising that he had created the dangerous situation, the defendant had a responsibility to limit the harmful effects of the fire. He could easily have done this by calling the fire brigade and his failure to do so left him liable for the damage.

■ The case also created the 'Miller principle' of contemporaneity.

***R* v *Mitchell* (1983)** (*constructive manslaughter*)**:** the *transferred malice* rule applies to constructive manslaughter.

■ The *defendant* had tried to push in nearer the front of a post office queue. An old man tried to stop him and the defendant punched him in the face, causing him to fall back and knock over an 89-year-old woman who subsequently died. The defendant was convicted for the constructive manslaughter of the woman, even though he had no *mens rea* towards her. The court transferred his *mens rea* from the man towards whom he did intend some harm to the woman who died.

***R* v *M'Naghten* (1843)** (*insanity*)**:** defines the defence of *insanity*.

■ The *defendant* suffered from paranoia and thought that the *government* was persecuting him. He decided to kill the prime minister, Robert Peel, but killed Peel's secretary instead. Medical experts gave evidence to the effect that the defendant was insane. There was a public outcry when the *jury* accepted this evidence and acquitted the defendant. This case led to the courts attempting to clarify the defence of insanity and their explanation became known as the 'M'Naghten rules', which have formed the basis of the defence ever since.

***R* v *Mohammed* (2005); *R* v *James*, *R* v *Karimi* (2006)** (*provocation*)**:** the *Court of Appeal* acknowledged that the decision of the *Privy Council* in *Attorney General for Jersey* v *Holley (2005)* was to be followed. As a matter of *judicial precedent*, the Court of Appeal is bound to follow a decision of the *House of Lords* rather than a conflicting decision of the Privy Council, but this was acknowledged to be an exceptional case.

***R* v *Moloney* (1985)** (*intention*)**:** the *defendant* and the victim (his stepfather) had been drinking heavily. They decided to have a race to see who could load and fire a gun in the fastest time. Moloney was quicker and pointed the gun at his stepfather who challenged him to fire it. Moloney promptly did so, hitting his stepfather in the head and killing him. At trial, Moloney claimed that he never intended to kill the victim or even to cause him serious harm, arguing that he was just joking around. The *House of Lords* substituted his *murder* conviction for one of *manslaughter*, stating that only an intention to kill or to cause serious injury was sufficient for a murder charge. It said the *jury* should ask if death or serious injury was a natural consequence of the defendant's actions. If so, it should then go on to consider whether the defendant realised this. If it believed that the defendant did realise this, this was evidence from which the jury could infer that the defendant did have the required intent.

R v Morris (1983) (*theft*): the *defendant's* assumption of any one right of the owner is sufficient to constitute *appropriation*. This means that touching someone's *property* is an appropriation, yet it is not theft unless the other elements defined in s.1 of the *Theft Act 1968* are present as well. In this case, changing the price of an item in a supermarket to that of a lower-priced item was considered to be an appropriation.

R v Nedrick (1986) (*intention*): the *defendant* held a grudge against a woman and intended to frighten her by pushing a lighted substance through her letterbox. Fire broke out in the house and the woman's child was killed. After a misdirection by the trial *judge*, the *Court of Appeal* said that the *jury* should determine whether the defendant had the required intention by asking first how probable the consequence was and second whether the defendant foresaw the consequence. If death or serious bodily harm were virtually certain to occur, and the defendant appreciated this, then the jury could use this as evidence that he had the necessary intention.

R v Pagett (1983) (*legal causation* — action of a third party): an unreasonable action of a third party may break the *chain of causation*.

■ The *defendant* was being chased by armed police. In order to resist lawful arrest, he took his girlfriend hostage. He then fired at police, using her as a human shield. The police returned fire and the girl was killed. Pagett tried to argue that he was not the cause of her death, but the court held that it was reasonably foreseeable that the police would return fire if shot at, so his conviction was upheld. The action of the third party (police) was not unreasonable and, therefore, it did not break the chain of causation.

R v Pembliton (1874) (*transferred malice*): during a fight outside a pub, the *defendant* threw a stone into a crowd of people, intending to injure them. Instead, the stone missed and smashed a window. The defendant was convicted of malicious damage, but this was quashed on appeal. The defendant had committed the *actus reus* of malicious damage but had the *mens rea* of assault, and since it was a completely different crime, the *mens rea* could not be transferred.

R v Quick (1973) (*non-insane automatism*): the *defendant* was a nurse. He suffered from diabetes and, while in a hypoglycaemic state, he attacked one of his patients. At trial, he said that he had taken his insulin but had not eaten and had also been drinking — all external factors. He had no recollection of the attack. The trial *judge* ruled that the correct defence was that of *insanity* and Quick then pleaded guilty. On appeal, his conviction was quashed and it was held that *automatism* should have been left to the *jury* — his condition had been induced by external rather than internal factors.

■ *TIP* If the case were to be heard today, Quick's condition might be regarded as being self-induced. This could have stopped him from relying on the defence of non-insane automatism.

R v *Richardson* (1998) (*consent*): the defence of consent may not be allowed if the *defendant* has obtained the victim's consent by fraudulent means.

■ The defendant was a dentist who had continued to practise despite being 'struck off' by the General Dental Council. She was convicted of *actual bodily harm*, but this was overturned on appeal. The *Court of Appeal* held that the patients had consented to be treated by her. They were aware of her identity and the nature and quality of the act that she was performing. It was not relevant that they would have refused consent had they known that she had been suspended.

■ Fraud invalidates consent only if the victim is deceived as to the identity of the defendant or the nature and quality of his or her act.

R v *Roberts* (1978) (*legal causation* — action of the victim; *actual bodily harm*): The *chain of causation* can be broken only if the victim does something unreasonable.

■ Late at night, the *defendant* gave a girl a lift in his car. During the journey, he began to make sexual advances, touching the girl's clothes. Frightened that he was going to rape her, she jumped out of the moving car, injuring herself. The defendant was held liable for her injuries, as they were a reasonably foreseeable result of his actions.

■ It was held that the defendant had committed the *actus reus* of a s.47 offence by touching the girl's clothing (*battery*) and this act had caused her to suffer *actual bodily harm*. The defendant argued that he neither intended to cause the ABH, nor had seen any risk of her suffering ABH as a result of his advances. This argument was rejected; the court held that the *mens rea* for battery was sufficient in itself and there was no need for any extra *mens rea* regarding ABH.

■ The actions of the victim were not considered unreasonable and therefore did not break the *chain of causation*.

R v *Robinson* (1977) (*robbery*): it is necessary first to prove *theft* before a charge of robbery can be considered.

■ The victim owed the *defendant* money. The defendant used a knife to threaten the victim. The victim dropped a £5 note that the defendant took as part payment of the £7 he was owed. The *Court of Appeal* quashed his conviction for robbery, as the *jury* at his trial should have been allowed to consider whether he was not acting *dishonestly* owing to the fact that he honestly believed he had a right in law to take the money (see s.2(1)(a) of the *Theft Act 1968*).

R v *Ryan* (1996) (*burglary*): the *defendant* was found trapped in a downstairs window, with only his head and right arm inside the building, and had to be freed by the fire brigade. He was convicted of burglary and appealed on the grounds that his *entry* had not been 'effective' as he was unable to steal anything on account of being stuck. The *Court of Appeal* upheld his conviction under s.9(1)(a) burglary, stating that it did not matter whether he could steal anything or not.

R v Secretary of State for Transport ex parte Factortame (1990): a case concerned with the power of the *European Union* and the loss of *sovereignty* of *Parliament* in the UK.

■ This case involved a Spanish fishing company that set up a business in the UK. Parliament passed the Merchant Shipping Act 1988 to prevent the Spanish fishermen from fishing in UK waters. This *Act of Parliament* was in direct conflict with the Treaty of Rome. The *judges* in this case applied the European Union law rather than the UK law. This case caused much controversy as it demonstrated the power of the European Union.

R v Shivpuri (1986) (*attempts*)**:** the *defendant* was arrested after being found carrying a suitcase that he believed contained either heroin or cannabis. In fact, the substance was merely dried cabbage leaves. The defendant was convicted of attempting to be knowingly concerned in dealing in controlled drugs. His conviction was upheld by the *Court of Appeal*. On appeal to the *House of Lords*, it took the opportunity to correct the mistake made a year earlier in *Anderton v Ryan (1985)*. It used the *Practice Statement 1966* to depart from its previous decision. The defendant was held to be guilty, since he had clearly intended to commit the offence and had carried out an act that was more than merely preparatory to the commission of the offence.

R v Slingsby (1995) (*consent*)**:** the *defendant* and the victim met at a nightclub. They engaged in various consensual sexual activities, during which the defendant's ring caused internal cuts to his victim. Neither the defendant nor his victim realised this. The victim's injuries later became infected and she died of septicaemia. The defendant was charged with *manslaughter*. However, he was acquitted, as the acts had been undertaken with the consent of the victim and he had not intended to cause injury, thereby lacking the relevant *mens rea*.

R v Small (1988) (*theft*)**:** the *defendant* took a car that he thought had been abandoned. There was much evidence to support this, in that it had been left in the same place for 2 weeks with its doors unlocked and the keys in the ignition. The car had a flat battery, no petrol and a flat tyre. The *Court of Appeal* quashed the defendant's conviction for theft, as it was up to the *jury* to decide if the defendant believed that the owner could not be found if he had taken reasonable steps.

■ This is an example of s.2(1)(c) of the *Theft Act 1968*, which gives some guidance as to what would not be considered *dishonesty*.

R v T (1990) (*non-insane automatism*)**:** the *defendant* was charged with *robbery* and *actual bodily harm*. At her trial, it transpired that she had been raped just a few days earlier and medical evidence was introduced to show that she was suffering from post-traumatic stress disorder as a result. She was said to be in a 'dissociative state' at the time of the offences and as such had not been acting consciously. The *judge* ruled that she was able to rely on the defence of non-insane automatism, since her state of mind was caused by the external event of the rape.

***R* v *Tandy* (1989)** (*diminished responsibility*)**:** the *defendant* was an alcoholic who strangled her 11-year-old daughter after the child had told her that the defendant's husband was abusing her. The defendant stated that she was able to exercise a degree of control over her drinking and her appeal against conviction was dismissed. To rely on diminished responsibility, the *abnormality of mind* has to be *induced by disease or injury*. The defendant had not demonstrated that her brain was damaged so she could not rely on 'injury'. In terms of disease, in order to rely on an abnormality of mind induced by alcoholism, the defendant had to show that her drinking was involuntary. As she admitted to having some control over her cravings and as her first drink of the day was voluntary, she was not able to rely on the defence.

***R* v *Thornton (No. 1)* (1992)** (*provocation*)**:** the court considered the concept of *cumulative provocation*.

- Battered women usually wait for an opportunity to attack their partners, and provocation was traditionally denied to them as they failed the 'sudden and temporary' *loss of self-control* requirement.

- After years of abuse at the hands of her husband, Sara Thornton stabbed him after he called her a whore and said that he would kill her. Her conviction for *murder* was upheld after the *Court of Appeal* agreed with the trial *judge* that her loss of control had not been sudden and temporary. She had gone into the kitchen to get the knife and had sharpened it prior to stabbing him. A second appeal was allowed in 1995 based on the concept of *battered women's syndrome*. Her murder conviction was reduced to *voluntary manslaughter*.

***R* v *Turner (No. 2)* (1971):** (*theft*) a person may be guilty when stealing his or her own *property*.

- The *defendant* took his own car from a garage that had repaired it, without paying for the repairs. He was found guilty of theft, as the garage had possession of the car, which amounted to a proprietary interest.

***R* v *Wacker* (2002)** (*gross negligence manslaughter*)**:** the *defendant* tried to smuggle 60 Chinese immigrants into the UK in his lorry. He closed the air vent in order to reduce suspicion. The immigrants suffocated in the back of the lorry and 58 were found dead. The defendant was found guilty of gross negligence manslaughter. Under the *civil law*, the defendant would not owe a *duty of care* because of the principle of *ex turpi causa non oritur actio*. This means that you do not owe a duty of care to people with whom you are carrying out an unlawful activity. The *Court of Appeal* stated that the civil principle of *ex turpi causa* did not apply to gross negligence manslaughter because it would be against public policy for it to do so.

***R* v *White* (1910)** (*factual causation* and *attempts*)**:** the *defendant* decided to kill his mother in order to benefit from his inheritance prematurely. He put poison in her drink, but before she consumed enough to kill her, she died of a heart attack. The prosecution could not prove that the defendant's actions were the factual cause of her death — 'but for' his actions she would still have died. Nonetheless, the defendant was still liable for attempted murder, as his actions were more than merely preparatory.

***R v Wilson* (1996)** (*consent*): the *defendant* used hot knives to brand his initials onto his wife's bottom at her request. Her injuries were reported to the police by her doctor and the defendant was charged with *actual bodily harm*. His conviction was overturned on appeal. The *Court of Appeal* held that the act was no more dangerous than tattooing and thus the defence of consent was available.

■ **TIP** The decision by the Court of Appeal in this case distinguished from the *House of Lords* decision in *R v Brown and Others* (1993).

***R v Windle* (1952)** (*insanity*): the *defendant* gave his wife a fatal overdose of aspirin. He said to the police: 'I suppose they will hang me for this.' This proved that he knew what he was doing was legally wrong, so he was unable to rely on the defence of insanity. His *murder* conviction was upheld by the *Court of Appeal*.

***R v Woollin* (1998)** (*intention*): the *defendant* lost his temper when his 3-month-old son started choking on his food. He picked him up, shook him and then threw him across the room towards his pram. The baby hit the wall instead and died as a result of his injuries. At trial, the defendant claimed that he had not intended to kill his son and had not wanted him to die. The *judge* told the *jury* that it could convict if it was satisfied that the defendant had seen a 'substantial risk' of serious injury. On appeal, the *House of Lords* confirmed that the consequence must be a virtually certain result of the defendant's actions and the defendant must appreciate this.

***Rylands v Fletcher* (1868):** a land-based *tort*.

■ The *defendant* mill owner wanted to build a reservoir on his *land*. He employed *independent contractors* to assess the land. The contractors discovered a disused mineshaft, but believed it was filled with earth. Unknown to the defendant or the contractors, this mineshaft connected to the *claimant's* coalmine on neighbouring land. When the reservoir was filled, water poured down the shaft and flooded the mine. The defendant had not been negligent, as he had trusted the independent contractors, yet he was liable for the *damage* to the claimant's land. This case created a new area of tort.

■ Blackburn J defined the rule as:

> A person who, for his own purposes, brings onto land and keeps there anything likely to do mischief if it escapes, must do so at his peril, and, if he does not do so, he is *prima facie* answerable for all damage which is the natural consequence of its escape.

Lord Cairns added that the use of land has to be 'non-natural'.

(1) The defendant must bring something onto his or her land for his or her purposes that does not naturally occur there (*Crowhurst* v *Amersham Burial Board*, 1878).

(2) A non-natural use of land must be made (*Cambridge Water* v *Eastern Counties Leather*, 1994).

(3) It must be foreseeable that the thing brought onto land is likely to cause mischief if it escapes. The escape itself does not have to be foreseeable (*Read* v *Lyons*, 1946).

(4) The escape must cause damage. The normal rules of *causation* apply (*Cambridge Water* v *Eastern Counties Leather*, 1994).

■ The claimant and defendant must both be *occupiers* of land (*Weller and Co.* v *Foot and Mouth Disease Research Institute*, 1966).

■ There are many defences including *volenti non fit injuria*, act of a stranger, statutory authority, contributory negligence and act of God.

■ *TIP* This tort has not often been used successfully because of the many elements that it is necessary to prove. In 1868, it was not possible for a claim to be made in the tort of *nuisance* for a one-off incident. Today, claimants who suffer such damage would probably make a claim under the law of nuisance or negligence. Despite this, *Rylands* v *Fletcher* survives and can be used in certain circumstances.

safeguards: see *police safeguards.*

scienter action: see *Animals Act 1971.* In common law, the owner of a tame animal was liable for damage it caused if he or she knew that it had a vicious tendency abnormal in the species.

***Scott* v *Avery* clause:** a clause included in the *contracts* of many businesses, which requires both parties to use *arbitration* should a dispute arise.

search at the police station: on arrival at the police station, a suspect is searched and the custody officer records any property. The police can remove anything that they reasonably believe the individual may use to cause physical injury to himself or herself or others, to damage property, interfere with evidence, assist the suspect to escape, or is reasonably believed to be evidence under s.54 of the *Police and Criminal Evidence Act 1984.*

■ Fingerprints and other non-intimate samples may then be taken (without consent if necessary). These include oral swabs, saliva, footwear impressions and photographs. A strip search or search of the mouth may be carried out if necessary to remove an article that a person would not be allowed to keep. This must be done by an officer of the same sex as the suspect.

■ Under s.55 of the Police and Criminal Evidence Act 1984, if a superintendent or superior officer has reasonable grounds for believing that the suspect may have concealed anything that he or she could use to injure himself or herself or others or may have concealed drugs, then the officer can authorise a qualified doctor or nurse to carry out a search of the suspect's bodily orifices.

■ Under s.62 of the Police and Criminal Evidence Act 1984, intimate samples, some of which require the suspect's consent, can be taken. These include blood, urine, semen, dental impressions, pubic hair and tissue.

secondary participation: the involvement of people in a crime who *aid, abet, counsel* or *procure* the *principal offender.*

■ These people are known as accomplices or *accessories.* They will be charged with the offence of aid, abet, counsel or procure if one of these four terms can be proved. It is stated in the Accessories and Abettors Act 1861 that:

Whosoever shall aid, abet, counsel or procure the commission of any offence…shall be liable to be tried…and punished as the principal offender.

S

secondary victim (*psychiatric injury*): secondary victims fear for the safety of others and are not in any physical danger themselves; therefore, the court is more reluctant to allow their claims. Certain claims are prevented by the 'control mechanisms' established in *Alcock* v *Chief Constable of South Yorkshire (1991)*.

second-degree murder: The *Law Commission* has suggested that the offence of *murder* should be divided into 'first-degree' and 'second-degree' categories. The proposed crime of second-degree murder would be used in cases where there was a:

- killing through an *intention* to do serious injury (even without an awareness of a serious risk of causing death); or
- killing where there was an awareness of a serious risk of causing death, coupled with an intention to cause some injury, a fear of injury or a risk of injury

■ Second-degree murder would also be the result when a partial defence of *provocation, diminished responsibility* or killing pursuant to a *suicide pact* is successfully pleaded to a charge of *first-degree murder*.

■ *TIP* The Law Commission proposals also include definitions of first-degree murder and *manslaughter*.

second reading (of the *parliamentary stage* of the *legislation* process): where the whole House debates the *bill*.

■ If there is a division, a vote is called. The MPs vote by passing through either the 'aye' door or the 'no' door. They are then counted as they return to their seats. The speaker will announce if the 'ayes have it', which means there is a majority of votes in favour of the bill. It will then pass to the *committee stage*.

■ The political parties use the '*whip*' system to ensure party support for an important bill.

select committee (*delegated legislation*): the group of MPs that scrutinises *statutory instruments* made by *government* departments.

■ The select committee will check the provisions of any laws made and can question the minister and his or her civil servants to make sure that they have not gone beyond the power given to them by *Parliament*.

self-defence: there is no liability for crimes committed in situations when *force* is needed to defend people or *property* or to prevent crime.

■ Self-defence is defined in the *common law* and by *statute*. Prevention of crime is covered by the *Criminal Law Act 1967*. Defence of property is regulated partially by common law and partially by statute, namely the *Criminal Damage Act 1971*.

■ For force to be justified, it must have been necessary. The *defendant* is judged according to the circumstances as he or she honestly believed them to be. To decide whether force was necessary, the *jury* will consider the surrounding circumstances (see *reasonable force*).

■ If a defendant makes a mistake and thinks that self-defence is necessary, he or she will be judged on the facts as he or she honestly believed them to be. This is still the case if the mistake was unreasonable (*R* v *Williams (Gladstone)*, 1984).

■ *TIP* Tight restrictions are needed to prevent people from taking the law into their own hands and the force used must always be justified in the circumstances (see *R* v *Martin, 2002*).

self-induced duress: the defence of *duress* will not be available where the *defendant* voluntarily became involved with criminals.

■ The defendant should have reasonably foreseen that he or she might be forced to commit crimes by threats or violence (see *R* v *Hasan, 2005*).

sentencing: a *judge* decides what penalty to give to those convicted of a criminal offence.

■ If someone pleads guilty or is found guilty after a trial, the *magistrates* or judge must decide what will happen to the person. The courts have a range of options open to them, including sending an offender to prison (*custodial sentence*) or requiring him or her to pay a *fine*. The option that is chosen will be based on many factors, including the type of offence, the minimum/maximum sentence available, the circumstances of the offence, the age of the *defendant*, his or her background and the aims of sentencing. Often, the court will order a *pre-sentencing report* to be compiled by the *probation service*. This looks at the offender and his or her crime in greater detail.

■ Aims of sentencing include: *retribution, reparation, deterrent, rehabilitation, protection of the public* and *denunciation*.

Sentencing Guidelines Council: *judges* from the *Court of Appeal* who decide the appropriate penalties for different crimes.

■ Most crimes have a statutory minimum and maximum sentence. The Sentencing Guidelines Council produced a set of guidelines to aid a *judge* when trying to decide a deserving punishment.

separation of powers: a theory put forward by the French political thinker *Montesquieu* maintaining that state power should not be in the hands of just one person or group.

■ According to the theory, power should be divided into three branches: legislative, executive and the *judiciary*.

■ The *government* has the power to suggest law, *Parliament* has the power to make it and *judges* enforce it. Each group acts independently and provides a check on the other two so that dictatorship and tyranny can be avoided.

■ It is important that judges are independent from pressure from the government and other sources, not only to ensure that trials are fair and are seen to be so, but also because of the constitutional idea of the separation of powers. Judges are difficult to remove, which means that they cannot be pressurised by threat of redundancy. The fact that judicial salaries are not voted for by Parliament also ensures that wages cannot be used as a bargaining tool. Judges are not allowed to sit in any case in which they have a personal interest — e.g. *Re Pinochet* (1999). Additionally, judges cannot be sued for decisions made and things done in their role as judge.

silk: a *lawyer* promoted to the position of *Queen's Counsel* is known informally as a 'silk', as he or she has earned the right to wear a silk gown in court.

sine die: Latin for 'without a date'.

■ This means a case is adjourned without a new date being decided.

sine qua non: Latin for 'without which it could not be' (also known as the *but-for test*).

■ *TIP* This is the requirement that the *defendant* is the factual cause (*factual causation*).

slander: see *defamation*.

slow-burn provocation: see *cumulative provocation*.

Small Claims Court: see *County Court* or *small claims track*.

small claims track: trials held in the Small Claims Court at the *County Court*, involving cases worth up to £5,000 (up to £1,000 for personal injury claims).

■ A *District Judge* hears the case with the *claimant* and *defendant*, and it is not necessary to have a *solicitor* present. It is a form of *arbitration* rather than *litigation*.

***Smith v Baker* (1891)** (*volenti non fit injuria*)**:** the *claimant* was employed by the *defendants* to work at a quarry. A crane would often swing heavy stones over his head while he worked. He complained to his employers about this, so was obviously aware of the risk, but this did not prevent him from succeeding in a claim for *negligence* when he was injured by a stone that fell from the crane. His employers could not rely on *volenti non fit injuria* as a defence to their negligence. The claimant had not consented to the harm merely by knowing about the risk. The *House of Lords* accepted that the claimant had little choice but to continue working in those conditions.

***Smith v Hughes* (1960):** an example of the *mischief rule* of *statutory interpretation*.

■ The *defendants* were charged with 'soliciting in a street or public place for the purposes of prostitution', contrary to the Street Offences Act 1959. They were soliciting from upstairs windows. Lord Parker used the mischief rule to convict, as he believed that the 'mischief' that *Parliament* had intended to stop was people in the street being bothered by prostitutes.

***Smith v Leech Brain and Co. Ltd* (1962)** (*negligence — damage*)**:** the *claimant's* husband was burnt on the lip because of the *defendant's* negligence. The burn caused cancer and he died. The burn was foreseeable and therefore the defendant was liable for the full extent of the husband's injuries, which resulted in death.

solicitor: a type of legal practitioner.

■ Solicitors are governed by the *Law Society*. They give initial advice to people with legal problems. They can also represent their clients in the lower courts. A solicitor may practise general law or specialise, and can form partnerships with other solicitors.

■ Solicitors may gain greater *rights of audience* by taking the Certificate of Advocacy. This allows them to represent their clients in the higher courts. Such solicitors are known as solicitor advocates. Solicitor advocates with the required number of years' experience are eligible to apply for all positions in the *judiciary*.

solicitor advocate: see *solicitor*.

sound memory (*Coke's definition of murder*)**:** as with other crimes, to be charged with *murder* the *defendant* must be sane.

■ See the defence of *insanity*.

sovereignty: power.

■ *e.g.* The sovereignty of *Parliament* means that Parliament is the supreme law-maker.

■ The sovereignty debate relates to the loss of Parliament's power when the UK joined the *European Union*.

***Spartan Steel and Alloys Ltd v Martin and Co.* Ltd (1973)** (*negligence — pure economic loss*)**:** the *defendant* negligently disconnected the power supply to the *claimant's* metal smelting company. The claimant claimed for:
(1) the *damage* to the metal that was being smelted at the time of the power cut
(2) the profits the company would have made from selling that metal
(3) future profits that may have been made during the time it took for the power to be restored and the vat mended

■ Lord Denning allowed the claim for points (1) and (2), but not for point (3). Point (3) concerns pure economic loss, which is not consequential to the original negligent act.

■ By limiting the responsibility of the defendant, the claimant cannot claim speculated profits.

special damage: see *public nuisance*.

special relationship (*omission*)**:** a relationship that gives rise to a duty to act.

■ Parents have a duty to look after their children and may be prosecuted if they fail to do so. The courts can also impose a duty even if the parties involved are not blood relations.

■ *e.g.* In *R v Gibbins and Proctor* (1918), a man and his common-law wife were living together with the man's 7-year old daughter. They failed to feed the child and the *Court of Appeal* upheld their conviction for *murder* when the girl starved to death. Both the father and his girlfriend were under a duty to act.

special verdict: if the defence of *insanity* is successful, it leads to a special verdict and the *defendant* will be deemed 'not guilty by reason of insanity'.

specific intent: a crime where the *mens rea* is *intention* only.

■ Examples of specific intent crimes are *murder, theft, robbery* and *burglary*.

■ *TIP* *Voluntary intoxication* and *involuntary intoxication* both provide a defence to specific intent crimes.

standard of care: see *breach of duty*.

standing committee: see *committee stage*.

stare decisis (of *judicial precedent*): Latin for 'to stand by the decision'.

state of affairs crime: where the *actus reus* involves 'being' rather than 'doing' — the circumstances surrounding the act make it an offence. The prosecution need only prove the existence of those circumstances (see *R* v *Larsonneur, 1933*).

■ *e.g.* For rape, it is not the sexual act itself that is a crime. It is the surrounding circumstances of the act — the fact that it was carried out without *consent*.

statute: see *Act of Parliament*.

statutory instruments: regulations made by *government* departments to implement the provisions made in *Acts of Parliament*.

■ Statutory instruments are a type of *delegated legislation*.

■ *e.g.* The Dangerous Dogs Act 1991 allows the home secretary to add more breeds of dangerous dogs to the Act if it is deemed necessary. The Department of Constitutional Affairs can make changes to the provision of *legal aid* under the Legal Aid Act 1998. The Department for Agriculture was able to close public footpaths during the foot-and-mouth outbreak in 2001.

statutory interpretation: the role of *judges* when they try to apply the law from an *Act of Parliament* to an actual case.

■ There are two approaches to statutory interpretation: the literal approach and the *purposive approach*. Judges who use the literal approach base their decision on the words used in the *statute*. Those who use the purposive approach look at more than just the words to find the purpose of the statute.

■ There are three main rules of statutory interpretation that judges use to decide a case. These are the *literal rule*, the *golden rule* and the *mischief rule*.

■ There are also three Latin rules of language (*ejusdem generis, expressio unius est exclusio alterius* and *noscitur a sociis*), as well as *intrinsic aids* and *extrinsic aids* that can be used.

statutory law: see *Act of Parliament*.

statutory nuisance: a *nuisance* that affects the environment.

■ The local authority regulates such nuisances (as opposed to private individuals bringing an action) and issues *abatement notices* to stop the nuisance; failure to comply can result in a *fine* being issued by the *Magistrates' Court*. Statutes that cover such nuisances include the Clean Air Act 1956, the Control of Pollution Act 1974 and the Environmental Protection Act 1990.

stop and search: the power of the police to question and search a person in a public place. (Also see *search at the police station*.)

■ The main police powers to stop and search are contained in the *Police and Criminal Evidence Act 1984*.

■ When a police officer requests a person in a public place to account for his or her presence, behaviour or possession of anything, a record must be made of this and a copy given to the person questioned. The record must include the date, time, place, reason why the person was questioned, the individual's definition of his or her ethnicity and the outcome. Refusing to answer questions may result in the suspect being charged with obstruction. The rules that relate to obstruction were decided in *Rice* v *Connolly (1966)* and *Ricketts* v *Cox (1982)*.

■ The power to search an individual also comes under s.1 of the Police and Criminal Evidence Act 1984 and is supplemented by Code A. A search occurs when the police stop an individual and search him or her, his or her clothes or anything that he or she is carrying. Code A states that powers to stop and search must be used fairly, with respect and without discrimination. An individual can be stopped and searched only if the police have reasonable suspicion that the suspect has drugs, weapons or stolen *property*, or things that could be used to commit a crime, an act of terrorism or criminal damage. The suspicion should be based on facts, intelligence, information or behaviour. It cannot be based on personal factors, including age, race, religion, appearance, previous convictions or generalisations, stereotypes or any of these factors in combination.

■ An individual must be informed that he or she is being stopped so that a search may be carried out. He or she must be informed of the officer's name or number and the station to which the officer is attached, given an explanation of the grounds upon which the search is being carried out and informed of the object of the search. If the officer is not in uniform, s.2(3) of the Police and Criminal Evidence Act 1984 states that he or she must provide identification.

strict liability (crime): strict liability offences are complete when the *defendant* performs the *actus reus*.

■ Such crimes do not require *mens rea*. Generally, the courts are not in favour of strict liability offences, preferring to find an element of fault before imposing criminal liability. Thus, most strict liability crimes are statutory in origin. There are some examples, however, of strict liability in *common law*.

■ *Regulatory offences* tend to be strict liability, e.g. traffic offences, health and safety offences and pollution.

■ There is always a presumption that *mens rea* is necessary for conviction of a criminal offence. This can be rebutted, however, with a 'compellingly clear' implication that *Parliament* intended otherwise.

strict liability (tort): liability for a *tort* that is imposed without the *claimant* having to prove that the *defendant* was at fault.

■ Most torts are strict liability. The burden of proving fault tends to be restricted to *criminal law* because of the severe punishments that may be imposed.

■ *Civil law* is concerned with *remedies* such as compensation and, as most people have insurance, it is not so vital to have the burden of proving fault.

S

- **e.g.** *Rylands* v *Fletcher (1868)* is a case involving a strict liability tort.
- **TIP** Although cases involving strict liability torts do not have to prove fault, they may still have to prove things such as foreseeability of *damage* or unreasonableness.

Sturges v Bridgman (1879) (*private nuisance*): the *defendant* owned a confectioner's that used machinery to manufacture its products. The *claimant* was a doctor's surgery that had never been affected by the noise and vibrations until it built an extension which was used as a patients' waiting room. The claimant was successful, as the *locality* was predominantly residential with many other doctors' surgeries. Therefore, the noise from the confectioner was deemed unreasonable, although it may not have been if the area had been predominantly industrial. The defence of *prescription* failed. The defendant's noisy machinery had been in use for over 20 years, but it became a *nuisance* only when the doctor extended his surgery closer to the defendant's premises.

subjective test: the court decides liability based on what it believes the *defendant* foresaw as the consequences of his or her actions.

- This test is more difficult to prove than an *objective test*. It is used in criminal law to establish the *mens rea* of the defendant.

substantial impairment (*diminished responsibility*): the *abnormality of mind* of the *defendant* must be significant.

- This is a matter for the *jury* to decide (see *R* v *Dietschmann, 2003*).
- The impairment need not be absolute so the defendant is without any responsibility, but it must be more than minimal. Thus, the defendant who knows what he or she is doing but who finds it extremely difficult to control his or her actions will be covered by the defence of diminished responsibility.

suicide pact: a partial defence to *murder* that reduces the charge to *voluntary manslaughter*.

- Section 4 of the *Homicide Act 1957* provides a defence to a murder charge for the survivor of a suicide pact.
- It must be proved by the *defendant* on the *balance of probabilities* that there was a suicide pact in existence and that all parties had a settled *intention* of dying throughout.
- **e.g.** A husband and wife may agree to commit suicide together. The husband may shoot his wife with the intention of killing her and then shoot himself. If his wife dies but he survives, he may then be charged with his wife's murder. In this case, he would be able to use the defence of suicide pact to reduce his liability to that of voluntary manslaughter.
- **TIP** Like *diminished responsibility* and *provocation*, this partial defence applies only to a charge of murder.

summary offences: the least serious 'petty' crimes.

- These are triable at the *Magistrates' Court*.
- **e.g.** *Assault* is a summary offence.

supervision order (*young offender*)**:** an order of the court ensuring that young offenders aged between 10 and 16 are closely supervised by social services or the *Probation Service* for a period of up to 3 years.

■ A range of conditions can be attached to the order, including *curfews* or residence requirements.

Supremacy of Parliament: *Parliament* is the supreme lawmaker in the UK.

■ *Statutory laws* must be applied by the courts and take precedence over any existing *common law* (i.e. law made by *judges*).

■ Since the *Human Rights Act 1998,* new *Acts of Parliament* should be compatible with it but will still be applied by the courts even if they are not.

■ The UK joined the *European Union* in 1973 and so must adhere to the European Communities Act 1972, which states that EU laws take precedence over UK *statutes.* Therefore, Parliament is no longer sovereign over European Union matters, although the UK could withdraw from the European Union if it so wished.

■ Parliament devolved some power to Scotland, Wales and Northern Ireland in 1998 but it remains sovereign.

Supreme Court of Judicature: a term used to describe the *High Court, Court of Appeal* and the *Crown Court.*

suspended sentence: see *custodial sentence.*

Sweet v Parsley (1970) (*statutory interpretation* and *strict liability*)**:** a teacher rented out her farmhouse to students who smoked cannabis on the *premises.* She was completely unaware of this, since she did not spend much time there. When the police raided the house and found the drugs, she was charged with 'being concerned in the management of premises used for the purposes of smoking cannabis'. She was eventually acquitted on appeal when the *House of Lords* held that any crime to which a social stigma was attached should normally require *mens rea.* Using the *literal rule* she was guilty of the offence, but Lord Diplock held that even though the *Act of Parliament* did not specify a *mens rea,* he presumed that one was necessary for this serious crime.

tagging: an electronic device is fitted to the offender's ankle to monitor his or her whereabouts while on *parole* or subject to a *curfew*.

tariff system: imposing similar sentences on offenders who commit similar crimes.

■ Sentencing guidelines are issued to the courts by the *Sentencing Guidelines Council*. The aim of the guidelines is to help to achieve consistency in sentencing. Courts are given a guideline sentence for an offence of a particular type, and they then consider any *aggravating factors* and *mitigating factors* before deciding upon the actual sentence.

■ The courts may prefer to impose an individualised sentence if the tariff system is not appropriate for a particular offender.

Ten-Minute Rule: a rule dictating the amount of time allocated to an MP who is trying to pass a *private members' bill*.

theft: defined in s.1 of the *Theft Act 1968*:
> A person is guilty of theft if he dishonestly appropriates property belonging to another with the intention of permanently depriving the other of it.

■ The *actus reus* of theft requires *appropriation* of *property* that belongs to another.

■ The *mens rea* of theft requires the *defendant* to be dishonest and to have an *intention to permanently deprive* the owner of his or her property.

■ *TIP* Theft is an *either-way offence* with a maximum sentence of 7 years' *imprisonment*.

Theft Act 1968: defines *theft* in s.1, *robbery* in s.8 and *burglary* in s.9.

Theft Act 1978: defines *making off without payment* in s.3.

thin-skull rule: if some pre-existing weakness or medical condition of the victim makes the result of an attack more severe than it would be ordinarily, the *defendant* cannot argue that the *chain of causation* has been broken.

■ This is also known as 'you take your victims as you find them' (see *R v Blaue, 1975*).

third reading (of the *parliamentary stage* of the *legislation* process)**:** the final read through of the *bill*.

■ There may be a short debate and a vote on any final changes to be made. The bill is then said to have 'passed through the House'. All the parliamentary stages will then be repeated in the *House of Lords*.

three-line whip: an MP must turn up to vote at the *second reading* of the *legislation* process. Failure to do so may result in the MP's party taking disciplinary action against him or her.

three-track system: civil court cases are allocated to either the *small claims track*, *fast track* or *multi-track*, depending on the type of case and the amount of money that is being claimed.

■ This system was created by *Lord Woolf* in the *Civil Procedure Rules 1999*.

***Tomlinson* v *Congleton Borough Council and Others* (2004)** (*occupiers' liability*)**:** the 18-year-old *claimant* was paralysed after diving into the *defendants'* lake and hitting his head on the bottom. The defendants had repeatedly tried to prevent swimming in the lake and there were signs stating that it was prohibited. Wardens regularly asked people not to swim and handed out leaflets to that effect. Although originally a *visitor* to the park, the claimant became a *trespasser* once he went into the lake, so the *Occupiers' Liability Act 1984* applied. The *Court of Appeal* found the defendants liable but on appeal the *House of Lords* overruled the decision. It was not the state of the lake that was dangerous, rather it was the actions of the claimant himself that were dangerous. As such, the defendants were not liable for his injuries.

tort: a civil wrong.

■ It includes civil laws such as *negligence, nuisance, occupiers' liability* etc.

■ Torts such as negligence are fault-based (the *claimant* must prove that the *defendant* breached his or her duty (*breach of duty*)), and some are *strict liability*, e.g. *Rylands* v *Fletcher*.

training contract: training undertaken by students who have passed the *Legal Practice Course* and wish to become *solicitors*.

■ This is usually 2 years' full-time practical experience in a solicitor's office, but it can also be with a *government* department, the *Crown Prosecution Service*, the *Magistrates' Court* Service or in-house legal departments. The trainee's time is usually spent working in various departments so that he or she gains practical experience in at least three different areas as stipulated by the *Law Society*, which regulates all training contracts. Training contracts are usually organised so that a trainee spends about 6 months in four different departments, although trainees may instead work in a variety of areas on a daily basis during the 2 years. Throughout the training contract the trainee is supervised by an experienced solicitor and the trainee's performance is reviewed regularly.

■ After completion of the training contract, the firm usually employs the trainee as a salaried solicitor, as long as a vacancy is available.

transferred malice: if the *defendant* forms the *mens rea* of a crime but commits the *actus reus* of the crime against someone or something else, the *mens rea* (or malice) is simply transferred to the actual victim.

■ This ensures that the defendant can be found guilty even though the actual result was unintended (see *R v Latimer, 1886*).

■ *e.g.* The defendant may intend to kill one person but makes a mistake as to his or her identity and kills a different person instead.

■ *TIP* The *mens rea* for one crime cannot be transferred to a totally different crime (see *R v Pembliton, 1874*).

treaty: the highest form of *European Union* law.

■ Treaties are primary *legislation*. They lay down the aims of the communities and create some rights and obligations.

■ Treaties are directly applicable, meaning that they automatically become law in the *member state* without the member state having to do anything.

■ Treaties also have a vertical and horizontal *direct effect* (see *Macarthys v Smith, 1979*).

trespasser (*burglary*)**:** someone who does not have permission or has gone beyond his or her permission to enter *premises*.

■ If the *defendant* has permission to enter premises, he or she is not a trespasser (see *R v Collins, 1973*). However, the defendant is a trespasser if he or she goes beyond the permission given to him or her (see *R v Jones and Smith, 1976*).

■ The defendant must either intend or be reckless that he or she is a trespasser.

trespasser (*occupiers' liability*)**:** someone who enters *land* or *premises* without permission.

■ It is possible for a person to enter land or premises as a *visitor* and then become a trespasser, e.g. if the *occupier* told his or her visitor to remain downstairs and the visitor then went upstairs, the visitor would be trespassing in that area.

■ *e.g.* See *Tomlinson v Congleton Borough Council and Others (2004)*.

trespassing livestock: livestock causing *damage* is governed by the *Animals Act 1971*.

■ Section 11 of the Animals Act 1971 defines 'livestock' as cattle, horses, asses, mules, hinnies, sheep, pigs, goats, poultry, deer that are not wild and captive game birds.

■ Liability for trespassing livestock is governed by s.4 of the Animals Act 1971. This states:

> Where livestock belonging to any person strays onto land in the ownership or occupation of another and (a) damage is done by the livestock to the land or any property on it which is in the ownership or possession of the other person; or (b) any expenses are reasonably incurred by that other person in keeping the livestock…the person to whom the livestock belongs is liable for the damages or expenses, except as otherwise provided by this Act.

t

trespass to land: an intentional or negligent direct *interference* with *land* in the possession of the *claimant*.

■ The trespass must be voluntary (*Smith* v *Stone*, 1647).

■ The claimant must prove that the *defendant* negligently or intentionally entered the land (*League Against Cruel Sports Ltd* v *Scott*, 1986). It does not matter whether or not the defendant negligently or intentionally trespasses, as long as his or her entry is intentional or negligent (*Basely* v *Clarkson*, 1682).

■ Defences include *volenti non fit injuria* (the claimant gave his or her permission for the defendant to enter the land), *lawful justification, necessity* or *jus tertii* (the defendant can prove that the land belongs to a third person rather than the claimant).

trespass to the person: a direct *interference* with a person's rights over his or her body or personal security.

■ Trespass to the person is actionable *per se* so the *claimant* does not need to prove any *damage* or injury, only that the *tort* has been committed. This is one of the oldest torts and it can be committed in three different ways — by *assault, battery* or *false imprisonment*.

■ Assault and battery are also criminal offences, but there is a civil remedy under this area of law.

triable either-way offence: see *either-way offence*.

tribunal: an alternative to court where a panel of three people will make a binding decision.

■ Domestic tribunals are used by professional bodies to discipline or resolve disputes within the profession, e.g. the *Law Society* governs *solicitors* and has the power to suspend or disbar a member for misconduct.

■ Administrative tribunals are set up by the *government* to allow citizens a way to challenge the decisions of powerful organisations. Such tribunals include rent tribunals, social security appeal tribunals, immigration appeals tribunals, mental health tribunals and, most commonly, employment tribunals. They are governed by the Tribunals and Enquiries Act 1992 and are supervised by the *Queen's Bench Division* of the *High Court*.

Tuberville v Savage (1669) (*assault*)**:** the *defendant* may make a statement that negates the threat.

■ Annoyed by someone's comments to him, the defendant put his hand on his sword, which by itself would have been enough to constitute an assault, but at the same time he said: 'If it were not assize time I would not take such language'. By this he meant that since *judges* were hearing criminal cases in town at the time, he had no intention of using violence. His statement negated the threat.

ulterior offences (*burglary*)**:** defined in s.9(2) of the *Theft Act 1968* as including *criminal damage, theft* or *grievous bodily harm*.

■ The *defendant* must intend to commit one of the ulterior offences to have the *mens rea* for s.9(1)(a) burglary.

ultra vires: Latin for 'beyond the powers'.

■ A case of *judicial review* is taken to the courts if it is believed that the *delegated legislation* has gone beyond the powers granted by *Parliament*.

■ There are two types of *ultra vires*:

 • Substantive *ultra vires* — the delegated legislation may be declared void if it allows something that the enabling Act did not intend, e.g. in *Commissioners of Customs and Excise* v *Cure and Deeley (1962)*.

 • Procedural *ultra vires* — the enabling Act may set out certain procedures that must be followed before the delegated legislation can be passed, e.g. *Agricultural, Horticultural and Forestry Training Board* v *Aylesbury Mushrooms Ltd (1972)*.

unlawful killing: the *actus reus* of *murder*.

unreasonable (*private nuisance*)**:** behaviour that goes beyond the normal bounds of reasonable conduct is considered a *nuisance*.

■ The court takes into account *abnormal sensitivity, locality, duration* and *malice*.

uplift fee: see *conditional fee agreement*.

utilitarianism: the theory that the greatest happiness for the greatest number of people should be the basis of law.

■ Utilitarianism tries to give a scientific and rational theory of law, as opposed to the *natural law theory* that is based on religion.

■ This theory is explained by *John Stuart Mill*.

verdict: the decision in a trial.
- In a criminal trial, the *jury* or *magistrates* will decide whether the *defendant* is guilty or not guilty.
- In a civil trial, the *judge* (or sometimes jury) will decide whether the defendant is liable or not liable.

vertical direct effect: see *direct effect*.

vicarious liability: legal liability for the *torts* or crimes committed by another.
- *e.g.* An employer is held responsible for torts committed by an *employee*.
- In order for vicarious liability to apply, the courts must ask two questions:
  - (1) Was the person who committed the tort employed by the *defendant*? (see *employee*)
  - (2) Was the tort committed in the *course of employment*?

video-link: a live video connection to the courtroom.
- A *defendant* may be allowed to make an appearance in court by video-link directly from a *prison* (where he or she is being held in *custody*).
- A vulnerable witness or victim may prefer to give his or her evidence via a video-link to avoid sitting in the courtroom. This is used particularly when children give evidence.

'Violence: Reforming the Offences Against the Person Act 1861': the Labour *government* produced the Draft Offences Against the Person Bill following this Home Office report.
- The bill created new offences:
  - clause 1: intentional serious injury
  - clause 2: reckless serious injury
  - clause 3: intentional or reckless injury
  - clause 4: *assault*
- The new sentences have stayed the same, with the exception of clause 2. This replaces s.20 *grievous bodily harm*, which used to carry a punishment of 5 years' imprisonment. The new clause 2 would increase this to 7 years' imprisonment. Sentences proposed are as follows:
  - intentional serious injury — life
  - reckless serious injury — 7 years

- intentional or reckless injury — 5 years
- Assault – 6 months

■ Clauses 1 and 2 will include only wounds that are considered by the court to be 'serious injury'.

■ Clause 1 is the only offence that can be committed by *omission*.

■ Intentional serious injury caused by disease would be allowed as a clause 1 offence. However, reckless serious injury caused by disease (clause 2) would not be allowed. This would change the current law in *R* v *Dica (2004)*.

■ The *mens rea* of *recklessness* used in both clause 2 and clause 3 would require proof that the *defendant* saw a risk to the injury that he or she actually caused. This changes the current law that recklessness only requires the defendant to foresee some harm (see *R* v *Roberts, 1978*, *R* v *Savage* and *R* v *Grimshaw*).

visitor (*occupiers' liability*): under the *Occupiers' Liability Act 1957* a *duty of care* is owed to a person who has permission to enter the *premises*.

■ A visitor may have *express permission* or *implied permission*. Anyone without permission is classed as a *trespasser* and the Occupiers' Liability Act 1957 does not apply. Instead, the *Occupiers' Liability Act 1984* contains the relevant provisions.

volenti non fit injuria (*civil law*): a Latin term meaning 'to a willing person, no injury is done' (*consent* of the victim).

■ *Volenti non fit injuria* operates as a complete defence and the *defendant* will not incur any liability. If the *claimant* has voluntarily undertaken the risk of harm, then he or she can have no claim against the party who inflicted it.

■ For consent to operate as a defence, it must be given freely by the claimant. Consent obtained by *duress* will therefore be invalid. The claimant must be aware that a risk exists and must understand the nature and extent of the risk.

■ Examples include a hospital patient who agrees to receive an injection or a boxer who agrees to take part in a boxing match. The patient would have no cause of action against the doctor who administered the injection, and the boxer would have no claim against his or her opponent. In both cases, they had voluntarily agreed to run the risk of the harm inflicted.

■ Consent can be either *express consent* or *implied consent*.

voluntary assumption of responsibility (*omission*): a duty to act may be imposed where someone voluntarily accepts responsibility for another.

■ *e.g.* In *R* v *Stone and Dobinson* (1977), the *defendants*, common-law husband and wife, were of low intelligence. After a visit from Stone's anorexic sister, they decided to take her in and look after her. Over the following weeks she became increasingly ill. She became confined to bed and eventually died of blood poisoning as a result of infected bedsores. The defendants were convicted of *manslaughter* and their convictions were upheld on appeal. They had voluntarily assumed a duty to look after Stone's sister, knowing that she was relying on them, and their failure to summon medical assistance had contributed to her death.

voluntary conduct: to be held criminally responsible for an offence, the *defendant* must have committed the *actus reus* of the crime voluntarily.

■ *e.g.* It would not be voluntary conduct if the defendant had a seizure and caused *criminal damage*, or if the defendant was forced to commit an offence (see *duress*).

voluntary intoxication: when the *defendant* voluntarily consumed alcohol or drugs commonly known to make people aggressive or out of control.

■ If the defendant is so intoxicated that he or she is incapable of forming the necessary *mens rea*, the defendant will have a defence to *specific intent* crimes but not *basic intent* crimes (*DPP* v *Majewski, 1977*).

voluntary manslaughter: a charge of *murder* will be reduced to one of voluntary manslaughter if the *defendant* successfully pleads one of the three partial defences (*provocation, diminished responsibility* or *suicide pact*).

■ Voluntary manslaughter was introduced by *Parliament* via the *Homicide Act 1957*. It was designed to cover situations where the defendant has the *actus reus* and *mens rea* of murder but the surrounding circumstances of the offence mean that the defendant's liability is reduced from murder to *manslaughter*.

■ *TIP* The defendant will not be charged with voluntary manslaughter but with murder, to which he or she will plead the relevant defence. If successful, he or she will then be convicted of manslaughter.

Wagon Mound (1961) (*negligence — damage*): a negligent oil spill from the *defendant's* tanker floated into Sydney Harbour. Sparks from welding ignited some of the oil and it set fire to the wharf. The defendant was not liable as this type of damage was not foreseeable.

■ This Australian case was decided by the *Privy Council* but has since been fully incorporated into the law of England and Wales.

warning signs (*occupiers' liability*): section 2(4)(a) of the *Occupiers' Liability Act 1957* states that:

> Where damage is caused to a visitor by a danger of which he had been warned by the occupier, the warning is not to be treated without more as absolving the occupier from liability, unless in all the circumstances it was enough to enable the visitor to be reasonably safe.

■ If an *occupier* gives his or her *visitor* sufficient warning of a danger so that the visitor is made reasonably safe, his or her duty is discharged. Whether a warning is sufficient will be a question of fact in each case.

warrant for arrest: a court order that allows the police to make an *arrest*.

■ The police must apply to the *Magistrates' Court* in writing and make an oral statement on oath. The police must have reasonable grounds to suspect that an imprisonable offence has been committed.

■ The warrant must name the person to be arrested and the offence.

■ Police who have been issued with a warrant may use reasonable force to enter and search *premises* in order to make an arrest.

Wednesbury unreasonableness: the courts will declare *delegated legislation* to be invalid when the law made under the enabling Act is 'unreasonable'. This was established in the case of *Associated Provincial Picture Houses* v *Wednesbury (1948)*. The Wednesbury Council imposed a restriction on cinemas that banned children under the age of 15 from being allowed entry. The courts considered this restriction to be unreasonable and declared it void.

■ *e.g.* In *R* v *Sacupima ex parte Newham London Borough Council* (2000), Newham Council offered people who had become homeless bed-and-breakfast accommodation in Brighton. These people would not be able to afford to stay in Brighton when they had to return to Newham for their benefits, schooling and medical treatment. The decision to rehouse them so far away was held to be unreasonable.

whips: MPs who try to ensure the support of the other members of their party when voting at the *second reading* of the *legislation* process.

■ Each party will issue a one-, two- or *three-line whip* to indicate the importance of the vote.

■ A three-line whip indicates that an MP must turn up to vote. Failure to do so may result in the MP's party taking disciplinary action against him or her.

■ *TIP* A free vote is usually allowed for controversial issues, *private members' bills* and to gauge the opinion of the whole of the *House of Commons*. This allows MPs to vote according to their personal opinions rather than how their party wishes them to vote.

White and Others v Chief Constable of South Yorkshire (1999) (*psychiatric injury — rescuers*): the rescuer must be in danger personally in order to claim for psychiatric injury.

■ The *claimants* were policemen who were involved in the Hillsborough disaster, in which 95 football supporters were crushed to death at a football match. The policemen took part in the attempted rescue, resuscitation and removal of the dead and seriously injured. They suffered post-traumatic stress disorder as a result. The *House of Lords* did not allow their claims as none of them were exposed to danger during the incident. Since this case, rescuers who were not in any personal danger are to be treated no differently from *secondary victims*.

White Paper (*legislation*): produced at the *consultation stage* of the *legislation* process.

■ The finalised version of the idea for a new law is produced as a White Paper, which is the *government's* 'statement of intent'.

will: a document that directs the distribution of a person's *property* on his or her death.

■ A will must be witnessed by two people and signed by the testator (the person making the will). The people named in the will are known as *beneficiaries* and there may be an executor appointed to take charge of the allocation of the will.

willingness to pay (*theft*): according to the *Theft Act 1968*, a *defendant's* willingness to pay does not necessarily mean that he or she was not acting dishonestly.

Wilsher v Essex Area Health Authority (1988) (*negligence — damage*): the *claimant* had gone blind. Medical evidence showed that there were six possible causes of the blindness. The doctor's negligence had been only one of the possible causes, so the doctor was not negligent.

witness: a person called to court to give evidence at a trial.

Wolfenden Report: see *Hart–Devlin debate*.

Woolf: see *Lord Woolf*.

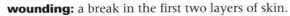

W

wounding: a break in the first two layers of skin.

■ Wounding is referred to in both s.20 and s.18 of the *Offences Against the Person Act 1861* (*grievous bodily harm*).

■ Internal bleeding or bruising does not constitute a wound (*C* v *Eisenhower*, 1984).

written constitution: a legal document that contains the rights of citizens and powers of *government* in a country.

■ A constitution is usually entrenched, which means it can be changed only by a special procedure. Countries usually write a constitution after a civil war (e.g. USA) or revolution (e.g. France).

■ The UK does not have a written constitution. There are no documents outlining the rights of citizens and the power of government. Instead, there are several documents such as the *Human Rights Act 1998* that outline the UK constitution.

■ *Dicey's rule of law* suggests that a written constitution is too rigid and does not allow the law to develop.

year and a day (*Coke's definition of murder*)**:** the former requirement that the victim must die of his or her injuries within a year and a day.

■ This rule was abolished by the *Law Reform (Year and a Day Rule) Act 1996*. As a result of advances in medical technology, doctors are now able to keep patients alive for much longer.

■ *TIP* Long breaks between the *defendant's* conduct and the victim's death make it difficult for the prosecution to prove *causation*.

young offender: a person under 18 years old who commits a crime.

■ When sentencing a young offender, the *judge* can impose a conditional or absolute *discharge* as well as a *fine*. There are differences, however, between *community sentences* and *custodial sentences* given to adults and those given to youths.

■ As well as the usual community sentences, such as a community rehabilitation order or a community punishment order, young offenders can also be sentenced to a *reparation order, referral order, attendance centre order, action plan order* or a *supervision order*.

young offenders' institution: offenders under the age of 18 cannot be given a *custodial sentence*, but they may be detained in a young offenders' institution or local authority accommodation.

■ A detention and training order can be given to those aged between 12 and 17, which sentences them for a period of between 4 months and 2 years. The first half of the sentence is spent in *custody*, while the second half is spent in the community under the supervision of the youth offending team.

■ Detention under sections 90 and 91 of the Powers of Criminal Courts (Sentencing) Act 2000 applies when a *young offender* is convicted of an offence for which an adult could receive at least 14 years in custody (e.g. *murder*) and can only be passed in the *Crown Court*. The youth will be kept in custody for any time up to the maximum limit that an adult convicted of the same crime could receive.

■ For sentences of less than 4 years, the young offender will be released at the halfway point and will then be under supervision up to the point at which three-quarters of the sentence has passed. For sentences of 4 years or more, the offender will attend a *parole* hearing and, if successful, he or she will leave custody at the halfway point of the sentence. If the offender is unsuccessful, he or she will leave at the two-thirds point. In either case, the offender will be kept under supervision until three-quarters of the sentence has passed.

Young v Bristol Aeroplane (1944) (*judicial precedent*)**:** this case established that the *Court of Appeal* is bound by its own previous decisions but with the three following exceptions:

(1) Where there are two previous Court of Appeal decisions that conflict, the Court of Appeal decides which to reject and which to follow.

(2) Where there is a conflicting *House of Lords* decision, the Court of Appeal must follow this and reject its previous decision.

(3) Where the previous decision was made *per incuriam* (carelessly or by mistake).

Youth Court: see *young offender* and *Magistrates' Court*.

zero tolerance: a policy of strict law and punishment.

■ This policy was first introduced in the USA in the 1980s in order to try to reduce drug-related crime.

■ Zero tolerance is used by the current Labour *government* to be tough on *young offenders*. One of the outcomes of this policy was the introduction of *antisocial behaviour orders*.